The Reference Shelf®

WITHDRAWN

U.S. National Debate Topic 2006–2007

National Service

Edited by Ronald Eniclerico

Editorial Advisor Lynn M. Messina

The Reference Shelf
Volume 78 • Number 3

The H. W. Wilson Company
2006

The Reference Shelf

The books in this series contain reprints of articles, excerpts from books, addresses on current issues, and studies of social trends in the United States and other countries. There are six separately bound numbers in each volume, all of which are usually published in the same calendar year. Numbers one through five are each devoted to a single subject, providing background information and discussion from various points of view and concluding with a subject index and comprehensive bibliography that lists books, pamphlets, and abstracts of additional articles on the subject. The final number of each volume is a collection of recent speeches, and it contains a cumulative speaker index. Books in the series may be purchased individually or on subscription.

Library of Congress has cataloged this title as follows:

U.S. national debate topic 2006-2007: national service / edited by Ronald Eniclerico.
    p. cm.—(The reference shelf; v. 78, no. 3)
  Includes bibliographical references and index.
  ISBN 0-8242-1061-1 (alk. paper)
  1. National service—United States. I. Eniclerico, Ronald. II. Title: National service. III. Series.
  HD4870.U6U82 2006
  362.973—dc22

2006009777

Cover: Matthew Nelson learns how to make a brick at Habitat for Humanity International's Global Village & Discovery Center June 7, 2003 in Americus, Georgia. (Photo by Erik S. Lesser/Getty Images)

Copyright © 2006 by the H.W. Wilson Company. All rights reserved. No part of this work may be reproduced or copied in any form or by any means, including but not restricted to graphic, electronic, and mechanical—for example, photocopying, recording, taping, or information and retrieval systems—without the express written permission of the publisher, except that a reviewer may quote and a magazine, newspaper, or electronic information service may print brief passages as part of a review written specifically for inclusion in that magazine, newspaper, or electronic service.

Visit H.W. Wilson's Web site: www.hwwilson.com

Printed in the United States of America

Contents

Preface vii

I. Historical Overview of National Service 1

Editor's Introduction 3
1) Cracking the Atom of Civic Power. Harris Wofford.
   National Civic Review 5
2) The Volunteering Decision. Paul C. Light. *Brookings Review* 23
3) New Directions: Service and the Bush Administration's Civic Agenda.
   John M. Bridgeland, Stephen Goldsmith, and Leslie Lenkowsky.
   Brookings Review 29
4) Suddenly Serviceable. Richard Just. *The American Prospect* 35
5) Volunteerism and Legislation: A Guidance Note. Inter-Parliamentary Union,
   International Federation of Red Cross and Red Crescent Societies,
   and United Nations Volunteers 39

II. Military Service and Conscription 61

Editor's Introduction 63
1) Rumors About a Draft Are False. Donald H. Rumsfeld.
   U.S. Department of Defense Web site (*www.defenselink.mil*) 65
2) Bring Back the Draft. Charles B. Rangel. *The New York Times* 67
3) The Case for the Draft. Phillip Carter and Paul Glastris.
   The Washington Monthly 69
4) An Army of the Willing. Richard A. Posner. *The New Republic* 82
5) Schroder to End Conscription in Push for EU Rapid Reaction Force.
   Tony Paterson. *The Sunday Telegraph* (London) 87

III. Youth and the Draft 89

Editor's Introduction 91
1) Considering the Draft. Max Friedman. *Winston-Salem Journal* 93
2) Well, No, They Won't Go. John Cook. *Chicago Tribune* 95
3) Young People Fear Return of Military Draft. Marian Gail Brown.
   Connecticut Post 99
4) Teens Frown on National Service Requirement. Dennis Welch.
   Gallup Poll Tuesday Briefing 101

IV. Community Service Programs 103

Editor's Introduction 105
1) Desire to Serve Stays for AmeriCorps Alums—Study: Members of Program Likely to Have More Civic Responsibility. David Tarrant. *The Dallas Morning News*............................. 107
2) AmeriCorps Steps Up, Digs In. Ken Leiser. *St. Louis Post-Dispatch* (Missouri) 110
3) Peace Corps Finds Renewed Passion in Volunteerism. John Faherty. *The Arizona Republic* 113
4) How UN Volunteer System Assists Kenya. Peter Mwaura. *Daily Nation* 116
5) Do the Nation a Service. John McCain. *Newsweek* 119
6) Denial of Service. Julian Sanchez. *Reason*............................. 121
7) Muting the Call to Service. Dave Eggers. *The New York Times*...... 123

V. Mandatory Universal National Service 127

Editor's Introduction 129
1) Monterey Bay Campus Is a Role Model. Eric Slater. *Los Angeles Times* 131
2) Kids with a Cause. Cathy Gulli. *Maclean's* 135
3) Uncle Sam Wants You. Alan Khazei and Michael Brown. *The Boston Globe* 137
4) September 11, 2001: The Case for Universal Service. Robert E. Litan. *Brookings Review* 139
5) A Bad Idea Whose Time Is Past: The Case Against Universal Service. Bruce Chapman. *Brookings Review* 145
6) Doing Disservice. Drake Bennett. *The American Prospect* 151
7) A Nation of Servants: Defining Public Service for the Twenty-first Century. Alan W. Dowd. *World and I* 155

Appendix 167
Statement Upon Signing Order Establishing the Peace Corps (Executive Order 10924). President John F. Kennedy 169
National Service Timeline. Corporation for National & Community Service........ 170

Bibliography 177
Books 179
Web Sites 181
Additional Periodical Articles with Abstracts 183

Index 191

Preface

As its title implies, this volume is intended to provide a reference point for those participating in the national high school debate over whether the U.S. government should pass legislation to increase the number of volunteers engaged in a wide variety of national service programs. Although the word "volunteer" suggests that such service would be optional, the question arises as to whether the United States should institute a mandatory national service program for high school or college graduates and what form that service should take. For instance, in addition to establishing more humanitarian programs, such as those involving social services, should the government reinstate the military draft? With the nation embroiled in ongoing conflicts in Afghanistan and Iraq, talk of a draft—while dismissed by Washington—has repeatedly surfaced among nervous teenagers and their parents.

This book organizes the debate over national service into five sections: The first discusses the history of national service programs in the United States, from initiatives instituted by Franklin Delano Roosevelt in the 1940s to those proposed by George W. Bush today. The next two chapters consider the prospect of a reinstated military draft, breaking the discussion into two sections: The first features commentary from analysts, professors, and government officials on both sides of the issue, while the second is concerned primarily with the views of young people, who, perhaps unsurprisingly, tend to oppose mandatory military service. The fourth chapter explores community service programs such as AmeriCorps and examines philosophical arguments over the governmental use of tax dollars to finance such endeavors. The final chapter directly confronts the issue of mandatory national service and includes arguments for and against a universal service program.

Throughout these chapters a more basic question arises from those on both sides of the debate: How much power should the state have over the daily lives of its citizens? Judy D. Whipps, writing in *Hypatia: A Journal of Feminist Philosophy*, identifies two competing ideologies, observing that "liberalism elevates one's personal choices and personal responsibilities," while "communitarianism highlights each person's responsibility to the communal welfare, a type of social commitment often missing from liberalism." Proponents of community service often describe it as a civic responsibility; according to Harris Wofford, writing in the *National Civic Review*, "What calls out the best from us is being asked to give of ourselves to something larger than ourselves." Opponents, such as Richard Posner, writing for the *New Republic*, refer to mandatory service programs, specifically conscription, as a form of slavery. If the government is able to demand that citizens engage in national service, are the people then, as Posner alleges, simply slaves of the state, or do their civil liberties require that the choice to serve be their own?

It is important to note that the debate over national service frequently crosses political lines. Although conservatives traditionally favor a decreased role for the federal government, President Bush has become a major proponent of government-mandated volunteer programs, while other Republicans, such as Senator John McCain of Arizona, have charged that the president has done too little to promote national service. Meanwhile, ironically, the driving force in the pro-draft movement has come from Democrats who oppose the government's current military operations in Iraq. In editing this collection I have tried to include as broad a spectrum of views as possible in order to encapsulate the principle arguments both for and against national service so as to provide a useful compendium of information on the topic.

I would like to thank all the authors and publications that have allowed the use of their articles in this compilation. I would also like to extend special thanks to Lynn Messina, Sandra Watson, Paul McCaffrey, and Richard Stein for their help and patience during the planning and production of this book; without them this collection would not have been possible. Additional thanks go to Dana Anhalt, Matthew Keitz, and my parents for their advice and support during the work on this book.

Ronald Eniclerico
June 2006

I. Historical Overview of National Service

Editor's Introduction

In his inaugural address on January 20, 1961, President John F. Kennedy issued a resounding challenge to the American people. By boldly proclaiming that Americans should "ask not what your country can do for you—ask what you can do for your country," Kennedy encouraged his fellow citizens to commit themselves to national service. Less than two months later, on March 1, 1961, Kennedy established the Peace Corps, which he described as a "pool of trained American men and women sent overseas by the U.S. Government or through private institutions and organizations to help foreign countries meet their urgent needs for skilled manpower." The Corps was the most significant national service program to be established since Franklin Delano Roosevelt's Civilian Conservation Corps (CCC). One of myriad New Deal programs designed to put unemployed Americans back to work during the Great Depression, the CCC was created in 1933, as Roosevelt's executive order reads, "for the relief of unemployment through the performance of useful public work, and for other purposes."

The goal of government-sponsored service programs is to provide citizens with the opportunity to assist communities in need, both domestically and overseas. Currently, the Corporation for National and Community Service, established in 1993 by President Bill Clinton, organizes and supports many of these initiatives, including AmeriCorps, the Senior Corps, and the Learn and Serve America program.

In "Cracking the Atom of Civic Power," Harris Wofford, a former U.S. senator and government official, details the history of national service programs from the end of World War II to the present. A strong advocate of such policies and a central figure in the establishment of the Peace Corps, Wofford focuses particularly on the early 1960s, when, he believes, the spirit of volunteerism reached its zenith, and on the Vietnam War era, when it was at its nadir. The impulse to volunteer was rekindled, he writes, when the Clinton administration established the Corporation for National Service, a body that Wofford served as CEO beginning in 1995. In Wofford's words, the purpose of the Corporation for National Service is "to bring the streams of service together in a rising river."

Paul C. Light offers a vivid contrast to Wofford's history, which focuses largely on Democratic presidents, in the subsequent article, "The Volunteering Decision," highlighting the contributions of Republican administrations in promoting volunteerism. Light contends that President Richard Nixon "may have boosted volunteerism more than any other president in modern history," and points to the Reagan administration's conservative belief that private initiatives would "accomplish far, far more than government programs ever could." Light also discusses methods of recruiting and maintaining sufficient numbers of volunteers, noting that ultimately, "little data suggests that presidents, past or present, have much weight when it comes to Americans' decisions to volunteer."

In "New Directions: Service and the Bush Administration's Civic Agenda," John M. Bridgeland, Stephen Goldsmith, and Leslie Lenkowsky praise President George W. Bush's support for national service programs in the aftermath of the September 11, 2001, terrorist attacks. While they acknowledge that Bush's attitude "no doubt surprised many people who had come to associate such efforts with Democratic presidents," the authors—all of whom were appointed to posts in national service programs by President Bush—remind readers of the "long tradition in American politics" that "warns against allowing government to encroach on the private sector."

Richard Just discusses the recent history of mandatory service proposals in "Suddenly Serviceable." In particular, he examines the decision by the Democratic Leadership Council (DLC), a centrist wing of the Democratic Party, to endorse a policy of universal service. Just writes that the decision was a difficult one that involved balancing several competing concerns, among them the fear that "A national-service program that was not compulsory ran the risk of becoming just another marginal outpost for volunteerism," and that "the idea of compulsory service ran contrary to the strong libertarian spirit of American culture and would no doubt be a hard sell."

The chapter concludes with "Volunteerism and Legislation: A Guidance Note," published by the United Nations Volunteers organization to reflect the philosophy behind the U.N.'s official International Year of Volunteers (2001). In addition to explaining the underlying rationale behind government measures to spur volunteerism, the article describes the existing statutes that regulate and promote service programs.

Cracking the Atom of Civic Power

By Harris Wofford
National Civic Review, Summer, 2005

Asked why he robbed banks, Willie Sutton said, "Because that's where the money is." Like Sutton perhaps, higher education may be short of money, but it is not short of brain and brawn. There is no better place to look for the human resources that cities need to meet the extra educational and social needs of children and families, or to help solve other critical problems, than America's four thousand colleges and universities. Their faculties, administrations, and trustees are more than a million strong, with connections to millions of alumni. The largest of the campus resources, right on hand to be called into action to help America's cities, is sixteen million students.

The most critical need—and the key to mobilizing the human and monetary resources to meet the needs of our cities—is educated, engaged, and responsible citizens who will work together to solve our communities' and our country's serious social problems. The largest deficit we face as a nation is the shortage of such active-duty citizens. In the brain and brawn of students, the campuses of this country offer the largest potential pool for such citizens.

This participation should not be deferred until the day after graduation. If higher education is to fulfill its mission, the practice of citizenship should be an integral part of civic education. Students are often proclaimed the leaders of tomorrow. It is more important for them to be seen as (and to see themselves as) leaders today. There is no more important way for students to develop and demonstrate their leadership—to be tested and to test themselves—than in action to help American cities. We need better education for millions of children who are at great risk. Children need Head Start and even earlier childhood education, such as Jumpstart; they need a healthy start, with health education and access to health care; they need extra tutoring in reading and mathematics; they need after-school programs with structure in a safe place; they need mentoring by caring adults; and, from the earliest age, they need age-appropriate forms of service learning.

It requires tremendous new resources for elementary and secondary teachers and nonprofit programs such as Boys and Girls Clubs, YMCAs, MENTOR, and after-school service and tutoring programs to provide that crucial assistance. Federal, state, and local govern-

---

"Cracking the Atom of Civic Power," by Harris Wofford. Copyright © 2005 John Wiley & Sons, Inc. Reprinted with permission of John Wiley & Sons, Inc.

ments are not able or willing to finance the hiring of enough new staff. To fill the gap, millions of volunteers are needed, either unpaid or with a modest stipend for service requiring a large investment of time (such as college work-study jobs, living allowances and education awards for AmeriCorps members, or various off-campus internships).

> *What calls out the best from us is being asked to give of ourselves to something larger than ourselves.*

Great goals can galvanize. What calls out the best from us is being asked to give of ourselves to something larger than ourselves. Asking college and university students to join in concerted, dedicated effort to turn around the lives of their younger neighbors in great trouble can be such a call to action. Ask, and they will go! In the process, they help our neighborhoods and cities solve one of their most pressing problems.

Civically engaged colleges and universities should take the lead in asking students and faculty to enlist in these efforts and together mobilize the other resources of their institution. This demands a quantum leap in engagement with cities and with the children of those cities. It requires a leap in leadership, first of all by presidents but also by trustees, faculties, and students. In this essay, I present an overview of the history of efforts to engage higher education and students in large-scale civic-engagement and service-learning programs in the hope of finding clues that will help us crack the "atom" of American civic power and produce a quantum leap in the civic engagement of America's campuses.

The Post–World War II Era

After the Second World War, my generation learned how American universities had secretly played a central part in producing the atomic bomb. In a metaphorical sense, our generation saw how the atom of American civic power was successfully cracked and harnessed to win a war we had to win. At the University of Chicago, where I went after coming out of the Army Air Corps, cracking the atom was more than a metaphor. The University's Stagg Field was the place where scientists produced the first nuclear chain reaction. We heard about the all-out, multipronged search for the way to build the bomb before Hitler did. In that war, all sectors of American society came together in the common cause, and we discovered what great goals can be achieved when this happens. We wanted to see it happen again—in winning the peace and solving important problems on the home front.

Many of my generation read William James's 1910 essay "The Moral Equivalent of War," which proposed a year or more of national service on the part of all young men to undertake some of the hardest tasks of the nation.[1] We had just done that and were not in a mood for further service, at least not then. Yet some form of that idea (usually including women) was in the air and stuck in the minds of many future leaders, among them John F. Kennedy and George H. W. Bush. We believed the intense experience of military service prepared us for civic leadership at home. Professors proclaimed us the greatest generation of students because so many of us had come out of the war with new curiosity and an avid desire to read and argue, and to explore the larger questions of how to choose a good life.

Chicago was a center of the atomic scientists' agitation for world nuclear control, and with the blessing of Albert Einstein our president, Robert Hutchins, formed a distinguished Committee to Frame a World Constitution. He became an eloquent and outspoken leader in the campaign for world government. He never preached civic engagement, but we were proud that he was himself engaged with vital and controversial public issues. When he spoke in Rockefeller Chapel, students packed the great hall to hear what he had to say (an experience most university presidents don't enjoy today). His subject was usually the world, but certainly not the city around us.

The urban problems of Chicago were very little, if at all, on our minds. No one asked us to become volunteers serving the city or the country. Nor was "service learning" an idea we had heard about unless we were reading John Dewey. Without demeaning our service in the military, we laughed at the line in Steinbeck's *The Grapes of Wrath* warning that "service" is what gas stations do to cars and bulls do to cows.[2] In fact, large metropolitan areas such as Chicago were dealing with increasingly difficult social problems and did need help. There was a huge migration into northern and western cities of poor black families from the South,[3] but it took another decade before the new U.S. Commission on Civil Rights, inspired by Fr. Theodore Hesburgh, president of Notre Dame, put the spotlight on the racial segregation of housing in the North. Those of us who staffed the commission's hearings on discrimination in housing found Chicago to be the most segregated community of all those we studied in the nation. But even in those years, we heard no call for universities and students to come to the help of cities.

The Sixties and the Peace Corps

The call did come in the 1960s. College students, like most Americans, were stirred by the words of the young new president who turned *ask* into an unforgettably strong verb. "The world is very different now," Kennedy began his inaugural address. "For man holds in his mortal hands the power to abolish all forms of human poverty and all forms of human life." He did not deal with any domestic issue, but at the last minute he added two words—"at home"—to an address wholly focused on the world. "The trumpet summons us," he said, "to a struggle against the common enemies of man: tyranny, poverty, disease and war itself," and committed America to support human rights "at home and around the world."[4]

In asking Americans to lift their sights to what they could do for their country, Kennedy's first call was to young Americans to volunteer in service overseas, in the one new program he proposed in his presidential campaign: the Peace Corps. University students played a crucial role in inspiring him to propose a Peace Corps at San Francisco's Cow Palace in the last days of the campaign. Then, after he was elected, college and university students helped turn the idea into a reality.

It was on the steps of the University of Michigan's Student Union in the middle of a cold night in mid-October 1960, in unplanned and extemporaneous remarks to some ten thousand long-waiting students, faculty, and townspeople, that Kennedy tossed out some leading questions: How many students were willing to spend ten years in Africa or Latin America or Asia? Or young doctors willing to serve in Ghana? To his undefined call to volunteer service abroad, the audience responded with extraordinary enthusiasm. In the next few days, 250 students and some faculty in a group they called "Americans Committed to World Responsibility" circulated a petition saying they would volunteer if a Peace Corps were launched. When the word got to Kennedy that nearly a thousand Michigan students had signed, he decided to spell out the idea and make it a major campaign promise.

After the election, more than thirty thousand college students and other mostly young Americans wrote to the incoming president supporting the idea, more mail than on any other subject. The National Student Association took up the cause and convened a national conference to help shape the idea. These were important factors in keeping Kennedy and his staff from forgetting the promise.

Sargent Shriver, who was asked to design (and later run) the new program, wrote that the Peace Corps would probably "still be just an idea but for the affirmative response of those Michigan students and faculty. Possibly Kennedy would have tried it once more on some other occasion, but without a strong popular response he would have concluded that the idea was impractical or premature. That probably would have ended it then and there. Instead, it was almost a case of spontaneous combustion."[5]

When by executive order President Kennedy boldly created the Peace Corps (even before Congress passed the authorizing legislation) tens of thousands of college students applied to be among the first volunteers. The report of Shriver's task force on the Peace Corps, which the president adopted and sent to Congress, proposed that "wherever feasible" the overseas projects themselves should be administered through contracts with colleges and universities, or through other nonprofit organizations operating overseas. There were already fifty-seven universities working, in thirty-seven countries, on economic development or education projects under contract with the U.S. aid program. As a practical matter, they were a constituency the Peace Corps needed. "As a high educational venture, the Peace Corps' proper carriers are our traditional institutions of higher education," the report sent to Congress stated. "It is time for American universities to become truly world universities."[6]

Kennedy, like Shriver, had a similar vision of the educational character of the venture. Through the Indiana Association of Universities, President Hesburgh of Notre Dame arranged for his university to organize and run the large program in Chile, which it did successfully for most of a decade with long-lasting impact on Notre Dame. But no other university or college rose to the occasion and sought to do so. Nor do I think Peace Corps administrators pursued others, although the Peace Corps contracted with a number of experienced universities to train volunteers for particular coun-

> *If higher education had embraced the Peace Corps as an integral part of its civic mission, we might now have several million former volunteers engaged in civic affairs at home and in shaping our relations with the world.*

tries. The plan sent to Congress called for the college and university channel, and administration by private agencies such as CARE, to be the preferred way but added that there would be some projects of a size, complexity, novelty, or urgency that could not be carried out, or carried out well, through such channels. Those familiar with the expansive appetite of government agencies will not be surprised that direct Peace Corps–run projects became the dominant, indeed almost the sole, model.

If we had gone the other way and higher education played a major part in developing and administering the Peace Corps—and used its effective lobbying power to win the necessary appropriations from Congress—the Peace Corps might well have reached the critical mass intended. On one of the occasions when, as his special assistant, I accompanied the president to the rose garden to send off a new contingent of volunteers, he commented afterward that this will be really serious when there are a hundred thousand volunteers a year—one million in a decade. Then, he said, for the first time we'd have a substantial constituency for an intelligent foreign policy. A large proportion of the 175,000-some volunteers who have returned in the last forty-two years were active-duty citizens, in their communities or in the country at large. If higher education had embraced the Peace Corps as an integral part of its civic mission, we might now have several million former volunteers engaged in civic affairs at home and in shaping our relations with the world.

If year by year a hundred thousand young Americans had gone for two years of service overseas, the contribution of the United States to the education and development of other nations would have been a matter of great pride on our part and appreciation by people around the world. It is mind-boggling to imagine the difference this might have made, or would now be making, in framing and implementing an intelligent American policy in the Middle East, Asia, Africa, and Latin America.

The War on Poverty

The early success of the Peace Corps soon led to formation of a domestic Peace Corps: the Volunteers in Service to America (VISTA). Before he was killed, Kennedy set in motion plans for an all-out assault on poverty. He also said that someday we must bring the Peace Corps idea home on a large scale. The new president, Lyndon Johnson, successfully used the shock of Kennedy's death to move the Congress and the country forward on both counts. Johnson declared "unconditional war on poverty in America" and appointed Shriver to direct it. He also called for doubling the Peace Corps, from ten thousand to twenty thousand. At the University of Kentucky in 1965, Johnson proposed that the nation "search for ways" through which "every young American will have the opportunity—and feel the obligation—to give at least a few years of his or her life to the service of others in the nation and in the world."[7] Shriver and Johnson saw VISTA volunteers as essential ground troops for the war on poverty. They would provide much of the people power for the other initiatives of the campaign: Head Start, Upward Bound, Job Corps, Community Legal Services, Foster Grandparents, and the community action programs in American cities. In creating those social inventions, Shriver drew heavily on the faculties of higher education. He called on college and university students to become full-time volunteers in VISTA, after graduation or as a working break during college or graduate school.

Recalling the speed and scale with which Franklin Roosevelt established the Civilian Conservation Corps (CCC) in his first hundred days in office, Shriver intended VISTA to grow with all practical speed to hundreds of thousands. He expected the Job Corps for high school dropouts and unemployed young people to match it.[8] The growth of the CCC in the 1930s was a precedent for such expectations.

When FDR found there were half a million young men out of school and out of work, he persuaded Congress to authorize a Civilian Conservation Corps of five hundred thousand. Selecting Col. George C. Marshall to organize the CCC camps, he asked the future leader of America's armed forces to get "those boys in the woods," and set a goal of a quarter of a million to be at work by the end of summer. By the end of July 1933, four months later, Marshall reported that there were more than three hundred thousand young men in sixteen hundred camps, working hard on long-needed conservation projects in our national parks and forests, and on other public land. By the time they graduated into military service in World War II, some three million men of the CCC had turned their lives around, while doing work that won lasting national acclaim.[9]

This was the kind of war Shriver wanted. The three forces of VISTA, Job Corps, and returned Peace Corps volunteers, he predicted, would become "a giant pincers movement converging in the great center which is smug and self-satisfied and complacent."[10] In a commencement talk at New York University (NYU), Shriver issued an appeal that he later took to many colleges and universities: "The poor for whom this university was founded are out in the night, in the street, in the overcrowded schools needing extra teachers, in the hospitals needing extra help, in the settlement houses needing volunteers. They need your help. We need men and women who will work in these programs and start new programs of their own. For this we need the manpower and the brainpower, we need the service of the colleges and universities of America." [11]

He called on NYU "and the faculty and student body of all other great universities to practice the politics of service here at home in your own neighborhoods—not by more courses in responsibility or in American social problems, not by lectures, not by commencement talks; but by political action in this true sense of politics, in the service of your city."[12] He asked them: "What kind of blood runs in your veins? Are you ready to practice the politics of service?"[13]

With nearly fifty thousand students and faculty, he said, "This university alone overshadows the whole Peace Corps in its resources and potential power. . . . An all-university project to end the cycle of poverty in the areas where you live and have your being is within the intellectual and spiritual power of this, the largest private educational institution in the world."[14]

If NYU did this "with all the resources at your command, then future generations will say that the problem of poverty was cracked, and that a chain reaction of progress was started here on University Heights and on Washington Square."[15]

In his memoirs, Johnson looked back with nostalgia on the electrifying beginning of the War on Poverty: "The excitement was contagious. Hundreds of people—high school and college students, returning Peace Corps men, housewives, and even congressional wives—volunteered to work thousands of hours in every kind of capacity. . . . They went at it with a fervor and created a ferment unknown since the days of the New Deal, when lights had burned through the night as men worked to restructure society."[16]

With the Vietnam War consuming more and more federal resources, the president and Congress started to cut back the plans for rapid expansion of VISTA and other antipoverty programs. Shriver was also disappointed with the response of academic leaders; neither NYU nor any other university made the major commitment he sought. It was another missed opportunity for higher education and the country.

Some cities nevertheless forged ahead under the leadership of determined and dynamic mayors. One of them, Republican John Lindsay of New York City, created an "urban Peace Corps" of young men and women, mostly college students, funded 80 percent by the federal work-study program. He also established an office for volunteers that became a model for other cities. According to personal conversations with a key organizer of Lindsay's Urban Corps, Stanley Litow (now president of the IBM International Foundation), the corps grew from a few hundred in 1966 to one thousand in 1969, to twenty-five hundred by 1970 when he became executive director, and by 1973 to nearly ten thousand participating college student interns mostly with work-study jobs when Lindsay left office. They worked part-time in the school year and full-time in the summer.

More than a hundred universities around New York had work-study contracts with the corps, and many cooperative education campuses such as Northeastern and Wilberforce sent students working for their co-op terms. The corps staffed health clinics with medical and dental students and the field offices for consumer affairs with law students. It sent other interns to tutoring programs and recreation centers. Except for a director and a few deputies in the mayor's office, the corps was entirely student-run. Its fiscal and job development and placement offices were all staffed with the interns.

The success of the Urban Corps was later recognized by the Ford Foundation, which started an Urban Corps National Development Office that helped scores of urban corps programs get started in other cities. In New York City, the corps continued for some years but was diminished in size and clout as federal work-study funds were reduced and colleges and universities increasingly sought to keep work-study jobs on the campus instead of students going out to serve in the community.

The Collapse of Hope

Before the sixties ended, the War on Poverty was abandoned as American resources—and young soldiers—were drawn into the other kind of war, in Vietnam. The controversy over that war itself produced unprecedented engagement in political action by students and faculty (and an occasional college president). Teach-ins, protest demonstrations, and on occasion civil disobedience (sometimes uncivil, even violent, disobedience) engulfed many campuses.

In the wake of the war and dwindling federal dollars, the wind went out of the sails of the idea of engaging millions of students and faculty in service to children and the cities. Though all the main antipoverty programs that Shriver started continue in some form to this day, none except Head Start reached anything like the scale envisioned. VISTA, for example, fell to less than five thousand (as did the Peace Corps, from its high in 1966 of nearly sixteen thousand).[17]

The sixties saw another form of civic engagement when tens of thousands of college and university students joined the civil rights movement as it came to a climax in the years of Martin Luther King, and college and high school students were often in the front ranks. The lunch counter sit-ins were started by black college students in the South, and the Student Nonviolent Coordinating Committee (SNCC), where John Lewis emerged as a national leader, was started by students and young graduates. White and black students from around the country answered the call to go to the dangerous frontlines of voter registration in the South. Some were beaten and jailed, and a few were killed. But the high hopes of that season of citizen action collapsed in the sad spring of 1968 as Robert Kennedy and Martin Luther King were assassinated.

Both King and Kennedy were pointing to the mountains of poverty and inequality of opportunity still to be climbed in the next stage of the struggle for full civil rights. Citing what Peace Corps volunteers were doing abroad, Kennedy called for young Americans "to take on the toughest jobs in this country, whether in a city slum, an Indian reservation or a mining town . . . to invest a year of their lives, at no salary and under Spartan conditions, to help millions of their fellow citizens who, through no fault of their own, are denied the essentials of a decent life."[18] As senator, he asked colleges and universities to join in helping transform Bedford Stuyvesant, one of the most depressed communities in New York City. To the angry cry of "Burn, baby, burn!" as riots raged in the cities, King said, "No, the right watchwords are 'Learn, baby, learn' and 'Build, baby, build!'" Instead of picking up the torch and carrying on in King's spirit, many young Americans, on and off campus, turned to a counterculture of drugs and civic disengagement. A depression set in, not of the economy but of the spirit, from which it has taken a long time for some, young and old, to recover.

A Period of Percolation

The hoped-for quantum leap in concerted action to end poverty and to enlist millions of young people in such action never materialized. Despite the lack of presidential leadership and loss of federal funds, however, many service and volunteer initiatives percolated up, from state and local communities, from colleges and universities, and from students and young people themselves.

In the late 1970s, another effort to secure federal funding for large-scale youth service got a serious hearing from the Carter administration. Recognizing the increasing number of urban young people dropping out of school or ending up on the streets, unemployed and without hope, President Jimmy Carter asked Vice President Walter Mondale to head a major task force on youth policy. The Committee for the Study of National Service (which I was then piloting) had just issued its report "Youth and the Needs of the Nation."[19] The committee's most respected spokesman, Father Hesburgh, and I presented our findings and recommendations to the vice president and found him responsive.

We were proposing a decentralized system of national service in which all young people would be challenged to serve full-time for one or more years in meeting the needs of the nation and the world community. Such service would not be required, but after proving itself we hoped the idea would grow "so that before long participation in either civilian or military National Service will be as generally accepted as going to high school."[20] We foresaw extensive involvement of colleges and universities as well as student organizations.

Mondale seemed keenly interested, and Carter's influential secretary of labor, Ray Marshall, and the chairman of the Joint Chiefs of Staff, Gen. David Jones, supported our proposals. President Carter's mother had been an enthusiastic Peace Corps volunteer in India, and the president himself was already a champion of volunteer service. For a while, there were signs that the president would propose some form of voluntary national service. Instead, Mondale's task force went the other way. With limited money available, they decided to focus entirely on helping poor and minority youth.

Thereafter, federal money was concentrated on job training, remedial education, and summer jobs for the disadvantaged. Most of the major foundations made the same decision. Some, such as the Ford and Pew foundations, however, did fund new demonstration urban youth service corps in a number of cities. Led by California and Pennsylvania, several states formed youth conservation corps on the model of Roosevelt's Civilian Conservation Corps. Started by Democratic Gov. Jerry Brown, the California corps grew to some two thousand corpsmembers and earned the support of all subsequent governors. The organizers of some of these youth corps wanted them to be "diverse" but with a twist: instead of the usual meaning—with substantial black and minority members—they hoped their corpsmembers would be black and white, college-bound as well as recent high school graduates and dropouts. But since almost all available funding was for efforts targeted on the disadvantaged, most of the corps soon became overwhelmingly black or Latino. That was also a twist on the old CCC, which was largely white and entirely segregated by race.

These corps often did outstanding work. Over the years, Youth-Build, a program led by a visionary War on Poverty veteran, Dorothy Stoneman, turned around the lives of thousands of young people who had dropped out of high school. They learned job skills and the value of hard work and teamwork while building homes for families in need. In 1984, these national, state, and local full-time youth programs joined to form the National Association of Service and Conservation Corps (NASCC), which grew to more than a hundred corps in thirty-seven states with twenty-three thousand young corpsmembers.

> *In the late 1980s, the idea of national service came back to life.*

On the front of traditional unpaid, part-time volunteering, the 1970s and 1980s also saw a steady increase in the number of volunteers and of communities that started volunteer centers. After he ran for president in 1968, former Michigan Republican Gov. George Romney became "Mr. Volunteer" and spent his later years building a network of several hundred such centers. Community service by volunteers of all ages grew through recruitment and placement by these local centers, by nonprofit organizations seeking volunteers, and by the continuing federal Retired Senior Volunteer Program (RSVP).

In accepting the Republican nomination in 1980, Ronald Reagan said: "Let us pledge to restore in our time the American spirit of volunteer service, of cooperation, of private and community initiative, a spirit that flows like a deep and mighty river through the history of our nation."[21] As president, however, he did little to make the river deeper and mightier.

In 1985, supported by leading college and university presidents, the Campus Compact was established at Brown University to build civic learning into campus and academic life through student service and all-round institutional involvement in the surrounding community. Under creative leadership, the compact through the years has worked effectively to deepen and make mightier the river of engagement and citizen service, and have it run through the heart of American campuses.[22] Best practices were shared, and a growing number of campuses became models of extensive student volunteering and effective faculty participation.

In the late 1980s, the idea of national service came back to life. The Democratic Leadership Council issued a landmark report, "Citizenship and National Service," recommending major investment in large-scale, full-time national service. Following the principle of reciprocity in the GI Bill of Rights, the council, with Arkansas Gov. Bill Clinton's strong endorsement, called for federal student aid to be conditioned on a year or more of service to the nation. The council's chairman, Sen. Sam Nunn, and Rep. David McCurdy introduced legislation to launch the plan. The bill was immediately attacked and sidetracked by many Democrats along with leading college and university presidents, who denounced it as unfair to poorer students since those who didn't need financial aid were under no similar pressure to serve.

Coming to the presidency with a vision of volunteer service as "a thousand points of light," George H. W. Bush appointed the first assistant to the president for national service, Gregg Petersmeyer; he proposed a new program for young people, Youth Engaged in Service (YES); and he set up the Points of Light Foundation and from the White House made daily "Points of Light awards." In 1990, he joined with Sen. Edward Kennedy and other legislators of both parties to enact the first National Service Act. Kennedy overcame opposition by turning from the stick to the carrot, providing new funds for service but with no service requirement attached to student aid.

The act created a bipartisan Commission on National and Community Service to promote voluntary service and service learning, with power to award demonstration grants to support a few full-time national service programs. One of those grants went to City Year, a program started by recent Harvard Law School graduates Alan Khazei and Michael Brown. They designed it to be a model of what national service might look like, with teams of black, white, and Latino young people, out of high school or college, working together for a year in demanding service in the city. I can report from personal observation that when Bill Clinton visited City Year's founding site in Boston during his 1992 campaign, he said, "The light went on and I knew that's what I want to do when I'm president."

The Twin Engines of Service

In 1993, when President Bush met with Clinton for their drive to Capitol Hill to the inauguration, the one thing he asked was that the incoming president "take care of my Points of Light!" Clinton agreed. Soon afterward, when his team under Eli Segal was preparing the new president's proposal for national service, many Democrats wanted to leave out any support for the Points of Light Foundation. In the Senate negotiations, those of us who favored joining the two initiatives prevailed. It was a winning combination; if partisanship had cut Points of Light we probably would not have secured the small number of Republican senators who made up the margin of victory for the new act.

The act turned the bipartisan commission into the Corporation for National and Community Service, with new resources and a mandate to bring the streams of service together in a rising river. It continued the long-standing senior volunteer programs (RSVP, Senior Companions, and Foster Grandparents) and made a modest appropriation for a Learn and Serve America program that included support for service learning in colleges and universities. The largest appropriation went to the new AmeriCorps, which was authorized to start at twenty thousand members. Despite vehement opposition by powerful Republicans in the House of Representatives, AmeriCorps, including VISTA, was to grow to fifty thousand by the turn of the century. Clinton called it "the transcendent idea" of his administration.

About one-third of AmeriCorps members had completed college or graduate school, one-third had some college, and one-third of them were just out of high school. About 10 percent had a Ph.D. or other professional degree and about an equal percentage were high school dropouts. Most of the grants for AmeriCorps positions were made and administered by bipartisan, governor-appointed state commissions, with college and university presidents often playing a leading role on those commissions. Many grants for AmeriCorps positions went to institutions of higher education or to organizations created and led by young people just out of college. Most of the assignments of AmeriCorps members were in urban programs of assistance to younger students and children.

Clinton called [AmeriCorps] "the transcendent idea" of his administration.

The stage was set for substantial further expansion when Mr. Volunteer, George Romney, proposed a summit convened by all the living presidents to turn the river of service into a truly mighty force. Instead of two competing streams of part-time voluntary service and full-time stipended national service, he had a vision of twin engines pulling together. He wanted their combined force to be the driving people power for an alliance of all the sectors of society to solve our most critical problems, at the top of which he put the plight of millions of youths.

In the summer of 1995, Romney presented to the president of the Points of Light Foundation, Robert Goodwin, and to me, as the newly nominated CEO of the Corporation for National Service, his case for what he called "a quantum leap in national service and community volunteering." In a memorandum he was trying to get to President Clinton, Romney wrote: "If we were threatened by external forces, our resurgence would be swift and sure, centered around a full-scale mobilization of the entire nation. Our domestic problems demand no less of a response than that same kind: a full-scale mobilization of all our creative resources from the largest corporation to the smallest neighborhood group. There are roles in this for government, business, education, religion, professional, civic organizations, youth and for each and every American."[23]

The summit did come to pass, with great fanfare, in Philadelphia in April 1997, but George Romney did not live to see it. It was convened by Presidents Clinton and Bush and attended by Presidents Carter and Ford, with Nancy Reagan representing her husband; it was chaired by Gen. Colin Powell and was organized by the Points of Light Foundation, the new National Service Corporation, and the United Way of America. Two thousand delegates came from 150 communities, with thirty governors, many mayors, CEOs of corporations and nonprofit organizations, religious leaders, college and university presidents, and students. The news media were there in large numbers and covered it in full force all weekend. The declaration signed at Independence Hall promised the kind of national and local all-sector mobilization Romney had dreamed of, focused on meeting the urgent needs of children and youth. Powell became chairman of the campaign called America's Promise: the Alliance for Youth. Until he became secretary of state, he carried the message across the country.

Romney would not have been happy to know how hard the mobilization of all the sectors of society, in all the major communities, proved to be. He had assumed that the moral and political leadership of the president of the United States was an essential ingredient for success, but President Clinton was embattled and could not give it authority or priority. Opinion polls showed Powell to be the

> **In ten years, AmeriCorps members have totaled more than 330,000, nearly double the number of Peace Corps volunteers after forty-four years.**

most respected of Americans. His leadership was crucial to the effort, but in 2001 he was called to another kind of national service. Government at all levels needed to give support, but it was (and remains) an excessively partisan time. Available resources for increased investment in the education of our children were severely limited by large tax cuts, increases in military spending, and, after September 11, 2001, more than $250 billion devoted to Iraq, Afghanistan, and the war on terrorism.

Nevertheless, through thick and thin many communities have maintained the community collaborations inspired by the summit, and the national America's Promise Alliance is moving into higher gear under CEO Marguerite Sallee. Organizations whose purpose is to provide the kind of help for children that was promised at the summit have grown. Boys and Girls Clubs have spread from two thousand to more than three thousand clubs, with new frontiers of service on Indian reservations and new clubs based in schools. Mentoring, through Big Brothers, Big Sisters, statewide initiatives of governors, and other parts of the MENTOR network, has gone from an estimated one-quarter million organized mentors to about two and a half million, with fifteen million more needed.[24]

The budget of the Corporation for National Service is now almost a billion dollars, most of it going to support work with children and youth, helping to fulfill the Five Promises made at Philadelphia. With CEO David Eisner, AmeriCorps has grown to seventy-five thousand members. In many programs, such as Habitat for Humanity, they have leveraged the expansion of traditional unpaid volunteering through their work of recruiting and coordinating volunteers. In ten years, AmeriCorps members have totaled more than 330,000, nearly double the number of Peace Corps volunteers after forty-four years. Campus Compact, well led by Liz Hollander, has grown to more than nine hundred member colleges and universities, with offices in thirty states and 280 full-time VISTA volunteers working in state and local programs across the country. With Project Pericles, Eugene Lang has opened another front in higher education with a special focus. Drawing on his long and dedicated chairmanship of the board of Swarthmore College, he has begun a determined effort to persuade smaller liberal arts colleges to take civic education and engagement from the periphery to the center of their curriculum and campus life.

After the September 11 attacks, President George W. Bush issued his own call for a quantum leap in civic engagement.

On the annual National Youth Service Day in April, organized by Youth Service America (YSA) and sponsored by State Farm and *Parade* magazine, more than a million young people and volunteers of all ages serve. It is now linked to Global Youth Service Day in more than a hundred countries. By zip codes, YSA's Website SERVEnet.org offers some forty thousand volunteer projects, each needing a number of volunteers. Competing with Youth Service Day to be the largest day of service is Make a Difference Day, sponsored actively by USA WEEKEND. The annual National Service-Learning Conference shows the growing strength of service learning at all levels of American education. It is convened by the National Youth Leadership Council and cosponsored by State Farm and YSA, bringing together more than two thousand teachers and professionals, with one-third students themselves. The Points of Light Foundation's annual Conference on Community and National Service, cosponsored with the corporation, is a similar sign of breadth and depth of the service movement. So is the response in cities and on campuses around the country to the congressional act officially making Martin Luther King Day a day of service—a day *on*, not a day *off*. In 2005, an estimated forty-five thousand volunteers registered for six hundred projects on King Day in greater Philadelphia.[25] The growing network of Hands-On and City Cares community organizations for civic action, based in Atlanta, is particularly appealing to young professionals in more than thirty cities.

After the September 11 attacks, President George W. Bush issued his own call for a quantum leap in civic engagement, asking all Americans to give four thousand hours, or two years, during their lifetime to service of their community and their country. He called for doubling the Peace Corps (with its two years of service), a twenty-five-thousand-member increase in AmeriCorps, and creation of a new Citizen Corps to enlist citizens in homeland security. To promote and coordinate these initiatives, he established the USA Freedom Corps as a cabinet-level coordinating body for all the streams of service. Launched by one of his close colleagues, John Bridgeland, it is advised by a Council on Service and Civic Participation, chaired by John Glenn and Bob Dole. Presidential awards are now under way for a hundred hours of service in a year (or fifty hours for children under fifteen). These awards for civic fitness are running parallel to the president's physical fitness awards. The president has sent a message to all schools in the United States asking them to engage their students in service learning, with a guidebook of suggestions for how to do it well. From the White House, the president and corporate leaders have launched a Business Strengthening America initiative, to add the power of corporate America to all these efforts.

A new White House Website, USAFreedomCorps.gov, affords one-stop access to all the major databases of volunteer opportunities. It offers information on all the president's initiatives and links to those of the Points of Light volunteer center network, the United Way, the Corporation for National Service, MENTOR, Volunteer Match, SERVEnet, and America's Promise. In a ceremony in the Rose Garden, President Bush signed the Philadelphia Declaration and committed his administration to support the promises to children and youth made at the Philadelphia Summit. First Lady Laura Bush, working with the chair of America's Promise, Alma Powell, has actively encouraged efforts to impart new impetus to the campaign to give all young people the fundamental resources they need to succeed.

In his 2005 state of the union address, the president proposed "a three year initiative to help organizations keep young people out of gangs and show young men an ideal of manhood that respects women and rejects violence." In announcing that the first lady will be the leader of this nationwide effort, he said: "Now we need to focus on giving young people, especially young men in our cities, better options than apathy or gangs or jail. . . . Taking on gang life will be one part of a broader outreach to at-risk youth, which involves parents and pastors, coaches and community leaders, in programs ranging from literacy to sports."[26]

If George Romney were with us today, he would be delighted with these presidential initiatives, so much in line with his vision for the summit. He would no doubt be impressed with the infrastructure of service that has been built. He would also call on the president, former presidents, and leaders of all sectors to give this cause the priority it requires to succeed. Romney was not one to rest content with just good incremental progress, and he would not yet find the kind of all-out mobilization for children and youth for which he yearned and worked. Gov. Mitt Romney said in his eulogy, "My father never succumbed to any of the childhood diseases—mumps, measles, chicken pox—and he never succumbed to any of the adult diseases—cynicism, apathy, and inaction."[27] As described by his son, George Romney would now be grabbing us and button holing us again for a renewed effort to crack the atom of civic power with his irrepressible hope of producing the quantum leap our nation needs.

Notes

1. James, W. *The Moral Equivalent of War*. International Conciliation, no. 27. New York: Carnegie Endowment for International Peace, 1910.
2. Steinbeck, J. *The Grapes of Wrath*. New York: Viking Penguin, 1939.
3. Lemann, N. *The Promised Land: The Great Black Migration and How It Changed America*. New York: Knopf, 1991.
4. Quoted in Clarke, T. *Ask Not: The Inauguration of John F. Kennedy and the Speech That Changed America*. New York: Holt, 2004, p. xiii.
5. Shriver, S. *Point of the Lance*. New York: HarperCollins, 1964, p. 11; Stossel, S. *Sarge: The Life and Times of Sargent Shriver*. Washington, D.C.: Smithsonian Books, 2004; Rice, G. T. *The Bold Experiment: JFK's Peace Corps*. Notre Dame, Ind.: University of Notre Dame Press, 1985.
6. Wofford, H. *Of Kennedys and Kings: Making Sense of the Sixties*. Pittsburgh: University of Pittsburgh Press, 1992, pp. 259–260; see also Wofford, H. "The Future of the Peace Corps." *Annals of the American Academy of Political and Social Science*, May 1966, vol. 365.
7. Quoted in Wofford (1992), p. 311.
8. Shriver (1964), pp. 18, 19.
9. McEntee, J. J. *Final Report of the Director of the Civilian Conservation Corps*. Washington, D.C.: Department of the Interior, 1942; *Roosevelt's Tree Army: A Brief History of the Civilian Conservation Corps*. National Association of CCC Alumni. Retrieved Mar. 7, 2005 (http://www.cccalumni.org/ historyl.html).
10. Wofford (1992), pp. 312.
11. Shriver (1964), p. 119.
12. Shriver (1964), p. 118.
13. Shriver (1964), p. 119.
14. Shriver (1964), p. 120.
15. Shriver (1964), p. 121.
16. Quoted in Wofford (1992), p. 288.
17. Dionne Jr., E. J., Drogosz, K. M., and Litan, R. E. (eds.). *United We Serve: National Service and the Future of Citizenship*. Washington, D.C.: Brookings Institution, 2003. See also *Brookings Review*, Fall 2002.

18. Quoted in Wofford (1992), pp. 289–290.
19. Committee for the Study of National Service. *Youth and the Needs of the Nation.* (Report.) Washington, D.C.: Potomac Institute, 1979.
20. Committee for the Study of National Service (1979), p. 2.
21. Reagan, R. "Time to Recapture Our Destiny." Acceptance address, Republican National Convention, July 17, 1980. Retrieved Mar. 7, 2005 (http://www.americanrhetoric.com/ speeches/ronaldreagan1980rnc.htm).
22. Campus Compact. *Season of Service and Essential Resources for Campus-Based Service, Service-Learning, and Civic Engagement.* (Annual report, 2003-04.) Providence, R.I.: Brown University, 2004. See also Harkavy, I. "Honoring Community, Honoring Place." *Campus Compact Reader*, Fall 2002; Ehrlich, T. (ed.). *Civic Responsibility and Higher Education.* Phoenix: Oryx Press, 2000.
23. Wofford, H., and Romney, G. W. Keynote address, Utah Conference on Volunteerism, Apr. 14, 1999, published by Utah Commission on Volunteers, p. 12.
24. See MENTOR/National Mentoring Partnership (www.mentoring.org) and the report *How Are the Children?* by America's Promise on the State of Our Nation's Youth, Alexandria, Va.: America's Promise: the Alliance for Youth, 2000.
25. Retrieved Mar. 7, 2005 (http://www.mlkdayofservice.org/).
26. Retrieved Mar. 7, 2005 (http://www.whitehouse.gov/stateoftheunion/2005/).
27. Quoted in Wofford and Romney (1999), pp. 8–9.

The Volunteering Decision

By Paul C. Light
BROOKINGS REVIEW, FALL 2002

George W. Bush is not the first president to ask Americans to give more of themselves to volunteering. Except for Gerald Ford, every president since John F. Kennedy has called for greater volunteerism. Some calls have been resonant, others barely audible; some have produced new federal agencies; others, private initiatives. But whatever the form, volunteering has been a staple of presidential agendas since 1961.

The Presidential Call to Service

Kennedy's call to service was the most eloquent and famous. Like Bush, Kennedy viewed volunteerism as essential to defending the nation in a time of great risk. "In the long history of the world, only a few generations have been granted the role of defending freedom in its hour of maximum danger. . . The energy, the faith, the devotion which we bring to this endeavor will light our country and all who serve it—and the glow from that fire can truly light the world. And so, my fellow Americans: ask not what your country can do for you—ask what you can do for your country." Kennedy's Peace Corps was the first in a long list of federal programs to promote volunteerism.

Lyndon Johnson followed Kennedy's lead in 1964 when he signed the Economic Opportunity Act creating Volunteers in Service to America (VISTA). He also helped create the Retired and Senior Volunteer Program (RSVP), the Foster Grandparents Program, the Senior Companion Program, and the Small Business Administration's Service Corps of Retired Executives (SCORE). But Johnson never issued a stirring national call to volunteerism; rather, he rooted his volunteerism in a handful of important, but small, federal initiatives. Ironically, of all Johnson's efforts to draw young Americans into civic life, the Vietnam War probably did the most—albeit through marches, rallies, flag-burnings, and demonstrations.

Richard Nixon may have boosted volunteerism more than any other president in modern history. Just four months into his administration, Nixon had created a Cabinet Committee on Voluntary Action and an Office of Voluntary Action within the Department of Housing and Urban Development and appointed a special

---

Article by Paul C. Light from *Brookings Review*, Fall 2002. Copyright © *Brookings Review*. Reprinted with permission.

consultant to the president on voluntary action. In November, he announced his "National Program on Voluntary Action" and then established the National Center for Voluntary Action, a nonprofit, nonpartisan private group, to pursue its goals.

Nixon also created an entirely new federal bureaucracy to administer the government's growing collection of voluntary programs. In 1971, he placed the Peace Corps, VISTA, the Foster Grandparents Program, SCORE, all the volunteer programs in the Office of Economic Opportunity, and the Office of Voluntary Action within a new agency called ACTION. In late 1973 he signed the Domestic Volunteer Service Act, giving ACTION greater authority to design and implement new programs aimed at a wider range of audiences.

Jimmy Carter—perhaps surprisingly, given his own recent work promoting Habitat for Humanity—did not make voluntary service a centerpiece of his presidency, although he did reorganize ACTION halfway through his term to give the Peace Corps greater autonomy.

Ronald Reagan established the White House Office of Private-Sector Initiatives in 1981 in the belief that such initiatives would "accomplish far, far more than government programs ever could." He said little more about volunteerism until 1986, when his May 24 radio address focused on the rising tide of volunteerism—"a reassertion of good, old-fashioned neighborliness now that our country has regained its self-confidence." The next day he joined in the first "Hands Across America" anti-hunger rally, which stretched across the nation.

George H. W. Bush was more Nixonian in his approach to volunteerism. He launched his "Points of Light" volunteering initiative in 1989 to call all Americans, including corporations, schools, and places of worship, to claim society's problems as their own and to help solve them. His call led directly to the creation of the private nonprofit Points of Light Foundation, which merged with Nixon's National Center for Voluntary Action in 1991 and is alive and active today. Together with other nonprofits, the Points of Light Foundation connects citizens to volunteer opportunities and dispenses advice and research on best practices to make those opportunities as meaningful as possible.

Bill Clinton also did his share to promote federally sponsored volunteer service, placing his National and Community Service Trust Act at the top of his first-year agenda. The resulting Corporation for National and Community Service administers the AmeriCorps volunteer service program, the Senior Corps, and Learn and Serve America; it also absorbed all the programs of ACTION. And in April 1997 Clinton joined former presidents Bush, Carter, and Ford—not to mention Oprah Winfrey—in the Presidents' Summit for America's Future in Philadelphia. The summit produced a new nonprofit organization called America's Promise to help children and youth.

Evaluations of Impact

George W. Bush's recent call for volunteerism fits comfortably within the tradition established by Nixon, Reagan, and his father. His focus is on the traditional notion that individuals should give to their communities out of the goodness of their hearts, not because of government inducements, though he acknowledges that inducements through programs such as AmeriCorps have their place in the volunteering regime.

Bush's call was unique in its specificity. He asked not just for community spirit, but for 4,000 hours of it. He set a measurable goal that every American can track by creating his or her own electronic journal on the Corporation for National and Community Service website. But Bush does not want just 4,000 hours of service. He wants Americans to get into the volunteering habit. Once past the first 4,000 hours, he hopes that volunteers will not stop.

Much as one can applaud the goal, however, little data suggests that presidents, past or present, have much weight when it comes to Americans' decisions to volunteer. According to the University of California, Los Angeles, Higher Education Research Institute, for example, the number of freshmen who reported any type of volunteering has been going up 1–3 percent a year since 1989, with little variation that might be attributed to presidential activism.

Little data suggests that presidents, past or present, have much weight when it comes to Americans' decisions to volunteer.

None of this means that presidents should stop talking about volunteering or supporting federal programs such as AmeriCorps. The Corporation for National and Community Service reported a dramatic surge in website visits following the president's State of the Union address. Online applications to AmeriCorps increased 50 percent in the month following the address, while the number of visits to the Senior Corps website jumped more than 130 percent.

But the research does suggest that something other than presidential goal-setting may be at work in prompting someone to decide to volunteer. Most important, it turns out, is making sure that volunteers are engaged by people they know and that their service allows them to make a difference.

The Service-Learning Effect

Ongoing research by the Higher Education Research Institute suggests that service learning has a powerful effect on volunteering. According to a January 2000 research-in-progress report, college students who enrolled in a service-learning course were particularly aware of the benefits of community service—probably, the authors surmise, because they discussed their service with each other and received emotional support from faculty. The study is based on a random sample of more than 22,000 undergraduates, most of whom entered college in the fall of 1994. Compared with students who did traditional community service, students in service-learning courses were more likely to develop a heightened sense of civic responsibility and personal effectiveness through their work.

All Volunteering Is Local

Parents, teachers, rabbis, and pastors may all have far greater sway over the decision to volunteer than presidents do. Presidents can certainly light the match, but others must fan the flame. The influence starts at home. A 2002 random-sample survey of 1,500 youths aged 15 to 25 conducted on behalf of the University of Maryland's Center for Information and Research in Civic Learning & Engagement (CIRCLE) found that young Americans who discuss politics at home are much more likely to register to vote, trust government, believe politicians pay attention to their concerns, and say they can make a difference solving community problems. In fact, dinner-table conversations about politics are more strongly related to volunteering than are traditional demographic variables such as race, sex, education, and income. As CIRCLE concludes, "Parental socialization affects both whether young adults volunteer, and how often."

The personal influence continues in connecting a diffuse readiness to volunteer with real opportunities. According to a 1997 random-sample survey of 1,002 youths aged 15 to 29 conducted for DoSomething, a national nonprofit that encourages community organizing, young Americans hear about volunteer opportunities with a community organization from a host of sources—advertisements (66 percent), friends or family members (59 percent), teachers (54 percent), posters or flyers at school (48 percent), specific organizations (48 percent), places of worship (42 percent), jobs (38 percent), coaches, scout leaders or other local leaders (33 percent), and groups to which they belong (30 percent). Obviously, there is plenty of chatter out there on volunteering.

But not all sources produce results equally. Forty-two percent of young Americans who heard about a volunteering opportunity from a direct source (friend, family member, coach, scout leader, teacher, or the organization itself) volunteered—as against only 14 percent of those who heard from an indirect source (place of worship, job or employer, posters or flyers, and advertisements).

And the more contacts from direct sources, the greater the results. Just 14 percent of students who never heard from a direct source said they volunteered, compared with 25 percent who heard from one source, 41 percent who heard from two, 47 percent from three, and 62 percent from four. Just as in the CIRCLE study, volunteering is clearly related to social networks. Having a parent who is, or was, involved in community activity, as well as being a young person who attends religious services regularly, also increases volunteer experience.

All volunteering, it seems, is local. Presidents can opine all they wish about the need for greater engagement, but parents, friends, and the volunteer organizations themselves get the results.

The Chance to Make a Difference

To get Americans into the volunteering habit, though, it will not be enough to ask them to volunteer—or even to get them to show up for a first experience. The service itself must be meaningful or the volunteers will not come back.

According to the DoSomething survey, young Americans respond to programs that make good use of their time. Volunteers want to make a difference—make key decisions, see the effects of their work, gain valuable experience, skills, or contacts. Half of the DoSomething respondents who made key decisions rated their volunteer experience as excellent, compared with just 29 percent of those who did not; 46 percent who could see the impact of their work also rated their experience as excellent, as against just 15 percent who could not.

Although a lack of time is by far the most important reason cited by most young Americans for a decision to stop volunteering, frustration and a lack of meaning may also diminish future engagements. Without question, for example, the quality of their volunteer experiences affects the way students view future jobs in charitable organizations. According to a May 2002 random-sample survey of 1,015 college seniors, students who volunteered and rated their experience as very positive and found their skills and talents very well used were more likely than others to consider seriously a career in the nonprofit sector. For example, 23 percent of students who felt their skills and talents were very well used said they had seriously thought about a job in the nonprofit sector, compared with 10 percent of those whose skills and talents were not used well at all, and 0 percent who never volunteered at all. To the extent that interest in work in the nonprofit sector can be used as a surrogate for future interest in volunteering, these data suggest that the quality of the volunteer experience matters.

According to the DoSomething survey, young Americans respond to programs that make good use of their time.

Strengthening the President's Call

If President Bush wants Americans, especially young Americans, to meet his 4,000-hour goal, he might broaden his agenda to include three provisions related to this research.

First, he should ask Congress for more funding to promote more service-learning opportunities at the primary, secondary, and college levels. The federal Learn and Serve America program should be highlighted for the largest increase in funding possible. Congress would be well-advised to change the AmeriCorps job description to include an explicit commitment to recruiting and connecting volunteers at the local level.

Second, the president might encourage his Corporation for Community and National Service to enlist parents, peers, and organizations to help advertise and promote volunteering. Although young Americans do pay attention to flyers and conventional advertising for volunteering, they respond best to direct appeals from the people and organizations they already know.

Third, and perhaps most important, the president should ask Congress to provide limited grants to make sure that volunteers are wisely used by the organizations they serve. According to Leslie Lenkowsky, the chief executive of the Corporation for National and Community Service, the success of any call to service "needs to go beyond massing forces to figuring out how to deploy them most effectively." One might add "and making sure they are wisely used." The federal budget includes no money to build capacity in the nonprofit sector or within faith-based organizations. President Bush may well encourage more volunteers to show up, but it is up to the organizations they serve to provide the work needed for a longer engagement.

New Directions

Service and the Bush Administration's Civic Agenda

BY JOHN M. BRIDGELAND, STEPHEN GOLDSMITH, AND LESLIE LENKOWSKY
BROOKINGS REVIEW, FALL 2002

From his first major speech as a presidential candidate, in Indianapolis in July 1999, George W. Bush has made expanding civic engagement and increasing the strength and effectiveness of civic institutions a central aim. He articulated his vision for an active and engaged citizenry in his inaugural address, in which he urged Americans to be "citizens, not spectators; citizens, not subjects; responsible citizens, building communities of service and a nation of character."

The events of September 11 added energy and urgency to this goal, as an active citizenry became an important bulwark against terrorist threats. These policy aims took their most concrete form in the 2002 State of the Union address, when President Bush called on all Americans to devote at least two years—or 4,000 hours—over their lifetimes in service to their communities, nation, and world. The president announced he had created the USA Freedom Corps to promote and coordinate government and private-sector efforts to give Americans more meaningful service opportunities to answer that call. As part of the USA Freedom Corps he also formed Citizen Corps to help citizens play appropriate roles in meeting the nation's emerging homeland defense needs and called for expanding the Peace Corps, Senior Corps, and AmeriCorps.

The president's embrace of national service programs, while springing directly from his philosophy of compassionate conservatism, no doubt surprised many people who had come to associate such efforts with Democratic presidents. Few people dispute that the voluntary efforts of citizens can make neighborhoods safer, the environment cleaner, children more prepared to face life's challenges, seniors healthier, and communities better able to deal with emergencies. But the challenge for many has been to define the role government ought to play in this arena. Can federally funded service be administered in a way that protects the independence of the civic sector and ensures that citizens, rather than government, take responsibility for the health and safety of their neighborhoods and their nation?

Article by John M. Bridgeland, Stephen Goldsmith, and Leslie Lenkowsky from *Brookings Review*, Fall 2002. Copyright © *Brookings Review*. Reprinted with permission.

Government and the Voluntary Sector

A long tradition in American politics warns against allowing government to encroach on the private sector. No less a student of American democracy than Alexis de Tocqueville warned that the growth of government could weaken the American tradition of joining civic groups. In the 1950s, sociologist Robert Nisbet, among others, lamented the decline of community, blaming it on the destructive effects of an expanding welfare state. Recently, a host of figures, especially Robert Putnam in his book *Bowling Alone*, have warned that Americans are reaching dangerous levels of civic disengagement, one measure of which is declining interest in volunteering and civic associations.

Not until 1965, however, did many thinkers who were concerned about government encroachment on the voluntary sector begin to develop a positive agenda for the diffuse web of nonprofit groups, associations, schools, and community organizations that came to be known as the "independent sector." Chief among them was Richard Cornuelle, a businessman and political activist, who in his 1965 book, *Reclaiming the American Dream*, challenged the right to demonstrate how private, nonprofit organizations could successfully tackle tasks such as making a college education affordable to the lower and middle classes, reducing poverty and welfare dependency, and improving housing for the needy. Could developing an agenda for the independent sector, he asked, offer a way to address pressing public needs without expanding government?

In Bush's vision, federal service programs fill a special niche—they create more opportunities for people to volunteer.

A decade later, two scholars from the American Enterprise Institute, Peter Berger and Richard John Neuhaus, set out such an agenda. They urged government to make better use of "mediating structures"—neighborhood, family, church, and voluntary associations—to deal with social problems. In their widely discussed "To Empower People," they set forth two propositions: first, that government policy should stop harming these mediating structures and, second, that it should use them whenever possible to realize social purposes.

During Governor Bush's campaign for the presidency, his support for mediating structures and the people they mobilize—now termed "armies of compassion"—figured prominently. He proposed to clear away legal and bureaucratic obstacles, thereby allowing the federal government to provide support to grassroots groups, exactly the kind of mediating institutions that Berger and Neuhaus had in mind.

In Bush's vision, federal service programs fill a special niche—they create more opportunities for people to volunteer. Through AmeriCorps, for example, the intensive commitment members make—up to 40 hours a week for one or two years—would be directed to helping organizations locate, train, and mobilize the armies of compassion.

September 11 and Service

In the fall of 2001, the administration was hoping to advance its strategy for citizen engagement through a "Communities of Character" initiative. The president was planning to spotlight places across the nation where people voluntarily came together to solve problems, putting others' interests above their own. The attacks on September 11 made that effort superfluous. Communities across the United States sent medical and relief teams to New York and Washington, while millions of ordinary citizens donated blood and money. "What can I do to help?" became an almost universal refrain, making citizenship and service more important than ever. In response, the president announced plans to increase the role of AmeriCorps members and Senior Corps volunteers in public safety, public health, and disaster relief and to focus their efforts more sharply on homeland security.

Service through the federal government is to strengthen, not replace, traditional volunteering.

In his 2002 State of the Union message, the two halves of the Bush administration's civic agenda came together. Toward the end of an address devoted chiefly to the war against terrorism, homeland security, and the economy, the president called on all Americans to devote at least two years during their lifetimes to serving their neighbors and their nation. Acts of goodness and compassion in one's community, he argued, would be an appropriate way of responding to the "evils" of September 11. And he proposed changes in national service programs to enable more Americans to serve both through these programs and through the grassroots organizations they would support.

These proposals represent a new direction in national and community service. To begin with, they put to rest the idea—which has gained currency in the aftermath of September 11—that national and community service should be made mandatory. Whether in AmeriCorps, the Peace Corps, or in private organizations, service, the president said, was to continue to be a voluntary, individual, moral commitment.

The proposed reforms also make clear that service through the federal government is to strengthen, not replace, traditional volunteering. The president anticipated that most Americans would answer his "call to service" by continuing to devote a few hours a week to work with a local church, school, hospital, or nonprofit. But federal programs like AmeriCorps and the Peace Corps would be available for those who wanted an intensive volunteer experience at home or abroad. The president also directed various cabinet departments to explore ways to encourage more Americans to volunteer and to remove any barriers to participation.

A New Role for Federal Service

In the administration's vision of national service, participants take on tasks different from those performed by ordinary volunteers. Volunteerism is not free, in the sense that volunteers must be recruited, organized, and set to work. To make more effective the efforts of millions of individual volunteers, who come to the table with all types of skills, abilities, and experiences, someone has to organize volunteer opportunities so that they meet concrete and clearly defined human needs. The organizations mobilizing the "armies of compassion" need corporals and sergeants—precisely the role that this administration sees for national service participants. Whether in education, the environment, public health, elder care, or strengthening homeland security, their long-term commitment is of special value to charities and public agencies, which can count on

> *The organizations mobilizing the "armies of compassion" need corporals and sergeants.*

them to show up each day, receive training, and take on long-range tasks and responsibilities that ordinary volunteers cannot—something known in the nonprofit world as "capacity building." That difference also justifies paying some of them a small stipend for living expenses, as well as a GI bill–type award for education.

Habitat for Humanity already follows this approach. It uses AmeriCorps members and Senior Corps volunteers to recruit, manage, and organize the traditional volunteers on which it relies to build homes for low-income people. Habitat founder Millard Fuller—once skeptical of AmeriCorps, but now an enthusiastic supporter—reports that volunteer leveraging by AmeriCorps members serving with Habitat has helped the group build 2,000 extra homes and engage more than 250,000 new volunteers. AmeriCorps members working with Habitat do not replace the volunteers who are building the houses; instead, they help recruit them from college campuses and elsewhere. They also ready the building sites so that when the hammer-swinging volunteers show up, they can get right to work and have a more productive experience. Along with helping Habitat build more houses, AmeriCorps participants thus engage more Americans in civic activities.

Another version of this model is to use AmeriCorps members to build the administrative and technological capacities of grassroots groups. For example, since it was created in 1965, members of Volunteers in Service to America (VISTA), who now make up about 15 percent of AmeriCorps members, have focused their efforts on mobilizing and managing teams of volunteer counselors, developing or expanding programs, and implementing administrative and accounting systems. Those efforts equip nonprofits—or voluntary public health or disaster relief groups—to do more of the work they already do. This fall, for example, VISTA will fund 10 members to work with Students in Free Enterprise (SIFE) at strategic points around the country, helping to develop SIFE teams that will teach financial literacy, from balancing checkbooks to investment strategies, to underprivileged populations in inner cities. The VISTA members won't do the actual teaching; rather, they will expand the program by training and developing new teams.

Implementing these strategies requires changing not only how federal service programs have been run, but also the laws establishing them. While VISTA members, for example, are allowed to do a wide range of capacity-building activities, other AmeriCorps participants, governed by rules enacted in the 1990s, are now required by law to provide services (such as tutoring or health

> *Americans can now find volunteer opportunities anywhere in the country (and even abroad) with just a few clicks of the mouse.*

care) directly to clients. Changes to allow national service participants to perform a wider range of services were incorporated in a set of principles for a Citizen Service Act, which the Bush administration unveiled last spring. The bill, which includes reforms to mobilize more volunteers who receive nothing from government, to make organizations receiving support more effective and accountable, and to remove barriers to participation in service programs, is now before Congress.

Finally, the president will use his new White House council, the USA Freedom Corps, to promote the health of the voluntary sector in general. The council will not only coordinate the efforts of all volunteer and service programs in the federal tent, but also concern itself with federal policies that affect the well-being of civil society. For example, it can work across federal agencies to improve the effectiveness of school tutoring programs that help students in need. And it can encourage organizations—businesses and nonprofits alike—to respond to the president's call to service by making institutional changes, such as giving employees paid time off for service, enlisting consumers in volunteer service activities, and increasing the capacity of service providers to use volunteers. For the first time, at the highest levels of our government, a presidential council will develop an agenda of "citizenship, service, and responsibility."

The USA Freedom Corps will link citizens with service opportunities in their communities. In July, the president unveiled a redesigned website (www.usafreedomcorps.gov) that features the USA Freedom Corps Volunteer Network, the largest clearinghouse of volunteer opportunities ever created. Thanks to an unprecedented collaboration among many government agencies, for-profit companies, nonprofit organizations, and private foundations, Americans can now find volunteer opportunities anywhere in the country (and even abroad) with just a few clicks of the mouse. The effort represents the power of government to rally diverse (and sometimes competitive) groups to a higher and shared purpose—and offers a glimpse of the public-private partnerships that are possible when government promotes service.

Since the president's call to service, interest in volunteer and national service is up. Key indicators include the increase in the numbers of citizens being matched with local service opportunities, as well as traffic at web sites for the USA Freedom Corps and the recruitment websites of Senior Corps and AmeriCorps, where applications have more than doubled. The Peace Corps also reports steady increases in applications. Nonprofit organizations, businesses, schools, faith-based groups, and other institutions are stepping forward to answer the call to service with new commitments and, in many cases, institutional changes that promise to foster a culture of service for years to come.

Service and Cultural Renewal

The Bush administration's civic agenda, together with its reform of national service, represents an unprecedented, cross-sector push to reconnect Americans to their communities and their country—and a new direction in how government views its role in strengthening the voluntary sector. Instead of bemoaning the decline of American mediating institutions, the administration seeks public actions to reinvigorate them. In an era of a high-tech, low-manpower military, it also looks for ways to involve as many Americans as possible in serving their country during a time of war and to encourage institutional changes at every level to ensure that volunteer service remains strong in times of peace. It aims to provide avenues for Americans, especially young adults and senior citizens able to offer sustained volunteer service, to dedicate themselves to reaching out and ministering to the needy and suffering. The president's service agenda clearly reflects the belief that citizens who are closest to the needs of people in local communities are best positioned to bring hope and help to those most needing it and that a renewed effort is needed to mobilize more Americans into volunteer service.

In identifying national and community service as a force for institutional and cultural renewal, the Bush administration has begun to make it an idea that Americans of all political stripes can embrace.

Suddenly Serviceable

BY RICHARD JUST
THE AMERICAN PROSPECT, JANUARY 1–14, 2002

For years, Charles Moskos has been churning out impassioned arguments for creating an American system of compulsory civilian and military service. The Northwestern University sociologist is widely recognized as the intellectual guru behind the national-service movement. But until recently, his idea seemed doomed to remain one of those noble proposals with almost no political appeal. It made antigovernment conservatives cringe and civil libertarians shudder. No one knew quite how it could be sold to the young people of America who would be asked to serve. Throughout the 1980s, it remained far outside the political mainstream, championed primarily by Moskos and out-of-power centrists at the Democratic Leadership Council. In 1990 the libertarian Cato Institute reported with evident relief that national service was "but a gleam in the eyes of a handful of philosophers and politicians."

Now with the new war on terrorism, national service has suddenly become a hot topic. Some commentators have called for reinstatement of the draft; others advocate an emphasis on civilian volunteerism. *The Washington Monthly*, a longtime proponent of national service, recently published a piece by Moskos and current editor-in-chief Paul Glastris calling for "a new kind of draft"—a version of which then popped up on *The Washington Post* op-ed page. And a bill in Congress sponsored by Arizona Senator John McCain and Indiana Senator Evan Bayh is winning a respectful hearing. The "handful of philosophers" that the Cato Institute worried about in 1990 has become more than a handful.

National service was one of the early animating proposals of the DLC. It drew sporadic interest from centrist politicians during the late 1980s. In 1988, while writing *Citizenship and National Service*—a booklet that became the blueprint for the DLC's position on the issue—Will Marshall, now the director of the DLC's Progressive Policy Institute, had wrestled with the question of whether to propose compulsory national service or, instead, a voluntary program of service opportunities for youths. It was a difficult choice: A national-service program that was not compulsory ran the risk of becoming just another marginal outpost for volunteerism. But the idea of compulsory service ran contrary to the strong libertarian spirit of American culture and would no doubt be a hard sell. Mar-

---

Reprinted with permission from Richard Just, "Suddenly Serviceable," *The American Prospect*, Volume 13, Number 1: January 1, 2002. The American Prospect, 11 Beacon Street, Suite 1120, Boston, MA 02108. All rights reserved.

shall's solution was to call for "universal" national service—a voluntary program appealing enough that young Americans would want to join, thus making national service a cultural rite of passage, though not quite a mandatory one.

The first significant step forward came following Bill Clinton's presidential-election victory in 1992, when advocates of national service finally had a sympathetic ear in the White House. AmeriCorps, a civilian community-service program that Clinton created in 1993 and modeled after the Peace Corps, would sponsor 50,000 service opportunities for young Americans per year—hardly the revolution some had envisioned but, says Marshall, an important "beachhead" nonetheless.

Given early Republican hostility in Congress, AmeriCorps might not have amounted to much more than a small experiment. But a funny thing happened on the way to the program's irrelevance: It began to succeed. Even skeptical Republican governors warmed up to it. When the maverick Republican presidential candidate John McCain started to champion the issue, it got an important boost.

McCain's candidacy crystallized a split between traditional conservatives and the group that had become known as national-greatness conservatives—among them writers, such as William Kristol and David Brooks of *The Weekly Standard*, and refugees from the far right, such as former Ralph Reed aide Marshall Wittman. One reason the issue was embraced, according to Brooks, is that in the ashes of the failed Gingrich revolution lay a new understanding that conservatives had to support a more dynamic notion of citizenship than mere commerce and private life—and national service filled that need well.

For his part, McCain had long been sympathetic to national service; he and Moskos had first met at a 1988 luncheon to celebrate the release of the professor's book *A Call to Civic Service*. While Timothy Noah was interviewing the senator about another topic in 1987, the conversation turned to a piece that Noah had written a year earlier for *The Washington Monthly* calling for a draft: "McCain said very straightforwardly that he believed in compulsory national service," Noah recalls. As the de facto leader of national-greatness conservatism, McCain began to sound themes in his 2000 election campaign that led advocates of national service to believe that they might have a new ally in their corner.

Marshall saw an opportunity: As the nation's attention focused on Florida in November 2000, he convened a summit. In attendance were members of the national-service establishment (John Gomperts of the Corporation for National Service and Alan Khazei of CityYear), their traditional patrons in the DLC (Ed Kilgore, the DLC's policy director, and legislative staff from Senator Bayh's office), and their new friends in the national-greatness movement (Kristol and Wittman, as well as a staffer from Republican Congressman Christopher Shays' office).

In the past, some national-service supporters had been most interested in civilian service; now, members of the Marshall group argued for an increased emphasis on military service as part of their joint initiative. "The civilian-service people," says Wittman, who attended as McCain's representative, were "very amenable to a military component." That first gathering brought the outlines of what would become the McCain-Bayh "call to service" bill into focus: quintupling the size of AmeriCorps over the next nine years, creating a new 18-month military enlistment option, and providing incentives for college students to perform community service. The group continued to meet; by the summer, the bill was almost ready.

> *The biggest challenge is convincing young people that national service is worth a year of their lives.*

Then tragedy struck—and a proposal that had looked innovative and ambitious on September 10 suddenly looked necessary, logical, perhaps even politically viable. September 11 tempered some of the ideological differences that had separated sectors of the national-service alliance. At the one pre–September 11 meeting he attended, Brooks says, "a lot there reminded me why I'm a conservative and not a liberal." He felt that some of the civilian-service positions being contemplated were unnecessary. But September 11 made it seem that there was no shortage of worthwhile civilian tasks.

Whether the political calculus has really changed for national service is another question, one that depends largely on whether the McCain-Bayh national-service expansion catches the imagination of young Americans. If it does, and only if it does, national-service advocates may be able to consider the ultimate goal—universal national service—within their reach. The biggest challenge is convincing young people that national service is worth a year of their lives. Jon Van Til, a Rutgers professor who has written extensively on civic service, says that the name recognition of AmeriCorps, among potential applicants and the public at large, is too low. If for no other reason than to give AmeriCorps the kind of cachet that would make it look good on a résumé—the kind of cachet the Peace Corps has—marketing the program aggressively must become a top priority.

Others point out that for national service to become a unifying rite of passage, elites will have to serve alongside everyone else. "If you did have prominent people—à la Chelsea Clinton—it might send ripples down the social ladder," Moskos says. On Marshall's desk at the Progressive Policy Institute is a photo of Elvis Presley in his GI uniform—a reminder, he says, that the burden of national service must be shared equally.

Alas, there is the problem of the military, which, ironically, has something of a historical antipathy to proposals like McCain-Bayh. "People in the military get a lot of expensive training, and it's cost-effective to try to get a fairly long return on that investment," explains Beth Asch, a senior economist who specializes in defense manpower at the Rand Corporation. "The services would be reluctant to have this be a major program." Short enlistments—as proposed by McCain-Bayh and endorsed by Moskos and other backers of the concept of citizen-soldiers—would address the socially dangerous gap between those who defend the country and those who benefit from their labor. But the military, Asch says, isn't interested in sociology; it's interested in defending the country. Short enlistments, she argues, don't necessarily help.

There is also continuing disagreement within the national-service movement as to whether the true goal should be compulsory service. Marshall and Brooks are not in favor of compulsory service; Glastris and Moskos, among others, are. The endgame for national-service advocates may or may not be restoration of the draft; but either way, it's a long road from quintupling the size of AmeriCorps and creating short enlistments to inspiring a generation and a nation—as McCain vowed to do this fall in *The Washington Monthly*. The AmeriCorps expansion sounds dramatic, but even with 250,000 slots, says David Hammack, an expert on nonprofits at Case Western Reserve University, "you're still not talking about a very large percentage" of Americans between the ages of 18 and 24 participating.

For his part, Moskos has no illusions about the prospects for making national service compulsory: He thinks they're slim, at least for now. (Not everyone does. "It may be sooner than we think," Wittman, the McCain adviser, says bullishly, "depending on what the needs are in this war." Glastris, too, is optimistic: "I think the draft would be terribly unpopular among a very vocal minority of Americans," he says. "But my gut instinct is that, in a qualified way, a majority of people would go for this.") Moskos knows that the draft may never be resurrected. But thanks to an unusual partnership—and in the wake of unexpected tragedy—he and his allies have managed to put their issue on the political agenda. The McCain-Bayh bill will likely be taken up by Congress early this year. If it passes, national-service backers will have their most expansive beachhead yet.

Volunteerism and Legislation

A Guidance Note

INTER-PARLIAMENTARY UNION, INTERNATIONAL FEDERATION OF RED
  CROSS AND RED CRESCENT SOCIETIES, AND UNITED NATIONS
  VOLUNTEERS
2004

I. Introduction

At the core of this Guidance Note are issues concerning the contribution of citizens to development, safety and social growth, and the desirability of recognising, valuing and promoting voluntary action by citizens in every country. Volunteering is a nursery for good citizenship. It helps build strong and cohesive communities. It teaches people to be responsible citizens and schools them in the process of democratic involvement. It promotes trust and reciprocity, which are essential to stable societies. The *Human Development Report 2002: Deepening Democracy in a Fragmented World* refers to volunteerism as holding enormous scope for broadening participation in governance and promoting more equitable outcomes for people.

The International Year of Volunteers, 2001 (IYV 2001), highlighted the existence of an enabling framework for volunteering as being one of the more important determinants of a flourishing volunteer movement. A growing number of countries, both industrialised and developing, have adopted or are considering adopting national legislation on volunteering. This Guidance Note on volunteerism and legislation (henceforth referred to as the Note) does not purport to cover all areas of legislation on volunteering nor is it a technical document with detailed consideration of each issue covered. It does, however, highlight the principal considerations in any legal framework, including recognition of the legal status of volunteers; the treatment of certain aspects of volunteerism under labour, social welfare and tax laws; the relationship between volunteers and volunteer-involving organisations; and legal provisions for the further development of volunteerism. It also respects the fundamental role of parliaments to enact laws and to have a direct impact on policies that support and promote improved livelihoods for all citizens, especially the more disadvantaged members of society. Finally, it needs to be emphasised that the Note is an advisory, not a prescriptive, document. It should be

---

Report by the Inter-Parliamentary Union, the International Federation of Red Cross and Red Crescent Societies, and United Nations Volunteers, 2004. Copyright © 2004. Reprinted with permission.

discussed among interested parties at country level, and a consensus should be arrived at as regards those elements which are likely to enhance the environment within which volunteerism can flourish in any given set of country-specific circumstances.

II. Forms of Volunteerism

Volunteerism is an ancient and global phenomenon. Since the beginning of civilization, a fundamental human value has been people helping people and, in the process, helping themselves. Most cultures have names to describe it: *Baranguay* in the Philippines; *bénévolat* and *volontariat* in France; *gotong royong* in Indonesia; *harambee* in Kenya; *shramadana* in India; *mingu* in Andean countries; and *al taawun wal tawasul* in many Arab States. The act is familiar even where the word "volunteer" is not.

> *Volunteerism is strongly influenced by the history, politics, religion and culture of communities.*

Volunteerism is strongly influenced by the history, politics, religion and culture of communities. What may be valued as volunteerism in one country may be dismissed as low-paid or labour-intensive work in another. Despite the wide variety of understandings, it is possible to identify some core characteristics of what constitutes voluntary activity.

First, voluntary activity is not undertaken primarily for financial reward, although reimbursement of expenses and some token payment may be allowed and even recommendable to facilitate access of individuals from all economic backgrounds. Second, it is undertaken voluntarily, according to an individual's own free will. Third, voluntary activity brings benefits to people other than the volunteer, although it is recognised that volunteering brings significant benefit to volunteers as well.

Volunteerism is about people helping, learning and actively participating in communities. Volunteerism has no borders. It is a cross-cutting social phenomenon that involves all groups in society and all aspects of human activity. It can take many different forms, depending on cultural and economic realities of countries and communities. Four expressions of volunteerism evolved out of IYV 2001.

Mutual aid in many parts of the world constitutes the main system of social and economic support. It often plays a primary role in the welfare of communities in developing countries, from small informal kinship and clan groupings to more formal associations and welfare groups. It also plays an important role in industrialised countries, particularly in the health and social welfare field, providing support and assistance to those in need.

Philanthropy or service to others is distinguished from mutual aid in that the primary recipient of the volunteering is not the member of the group him or herself, but an external third party, although most people would acknowledge that philanthropy includes an element of self-interest. This type of volunteering takes place typically within voluntary or community organisations, although in certain countries there is a strong tradition of volunteering within the public sector and a growing interest in volunteering in the corporate sector. There is also a long-standing tradition of volunteers being sent from one country to another to offer development and humanitarian assistance, both North to South and South to South.

A third expression of volunteerism is *participation* or *civic engagement*. This refers to the role played by individuals in the governance process, from representation on government consultation bodies to user involvement in local development projects. As a form of volunteering, it is found in all countries, although it is most developed in countries with a strong tradition of civic engagement.

Finally, *advocacy* or *campaigning* is a form of volunteerism which may be instigated and maintained by volunteers. It may include working towards a change in legislation affecting the rights of people with disabilities, or the introduction of anti-discrimination measures. Through advocacy and campaigning, volunteers have paved the way for the introduction of new welfare services in the field of HIV/AIDS, have raised public consciousness about human rights and the environment, and have been active in the women's movement.

This Note focuses on volunteering channelled through formally constituted volunteer-involving organisations from the voluntary or private sector, as well as through government agencies. However, volunteerism is also very dynamic, and different types of volunteer involvement are not mutually exclusive. Volunteers engaged in philanthropic or service delivery agencies may be involved in advocacy and campaigning as well as in mutual aid arrangements.

III. Legislation and Volunteerism

Until IYV 2001, few States had seen a need to pay attention to the legal issues which have an impact on the willingness and ability of citizens to volunteer. During the extensive preparatory work undertaken for the Year it became increasingly clear that the existence of enabling legislation may be in fact an important contributor to the extent to which volunteerism flourishes in any given situation. The United Nations General Assembly took up this theme and included legislation which encourages or inspires citizens to volunteer among the recommendations for supporting volunteering in Resolution 56/38, adopted at its 56th session, in 2001.

The context for this document is the widely recognised need, especially since IYV 2001, to clarify the nature of volunteer environments in the modern world.

First, as has been seen, volunteerism takes many forms and makes contributions in many different ways. It is also affected by many influences. These include socio cultural characteristics, the political system, economic structures and wealth distribution, institutional divisions of labour, beliefs and values, traditions and other principles and norms. Some of these features are defined in laws, but many are not.

Second, laws and statutes alone cannot fully define the environment for volunteerism. For by its very nature, volunteerism succeeds because of the wish of citizens to make their own contribution. Not only would the spirit of volunteerism be harmed if legislation were drafted with a purpose of control, instead of facilitation, but its very purpose would be distorted.

Third, there is a clear trend away from public sector involvement in many of the activities traditionally supported by volunteers. Parliamentary action should also aim to ensure that laws with specific purposes do not restrict opportunities for the enhancement of an enabling volunteer environment. It should also ensure that principles supporting volunteerism are understood and appreciated in

> *Not only would the spirit of volunteerism be harmed if legislation were drafted with a purpose of control, instead of facilitation, but its very purpose would be distorted.*

wide government circles, including at the local level.

In summary, legislation on volunteerism has to be approached with care and with openness as regards the social and cultural make-up of a given country and the governance systems in place. Legal reform should not be over emphasised at the cost of attention to the actual norms by which citizens choose to undertake voluntary action. Great care is needed, moreover, to ensure that legislation on volunteering is considered in full consultation with the principal stakeholders, especially from civil society, so that it is fully aligned with real needs and possibilities and does not create additional obstacles.

The core of the Note is divided into two sections:

Section A discusses the impact that different existing laws have on volunteerism, including: fundamental rights and freedoms, international law, labour law, tax law, social welfare laws, immigration law, and the regulatory framework for non-profit or charitable organisations. Suggestions on ways to promote a favourable legal framework for volunteerism are offered following the presentation of each of the different issues affecting volunteerism.

Section B discusses the need for laws which apply specifically to volunteer work. The Note will highlight the importance of having a framework law on volunteerism as a means to ensure, on the one hand, proper legal recognition for all forms of voluntary action, and on the other hand, appropriate treatment of the different elements of volunteerism under areas of law that currently affect its development. Suggestions are offered on legal provisions which can promote engagement in voluntary activity, drawing on existing laws and regulations on volunteering that are in force in different countries around the world.

A. Areas of Law that Can Have an Impact on Volunteerism

In the absence of a clear legal definition of what constitutes voluntary work and a volunteer, some laws and regulations can inadvertently have an impact on voluntary action. States should pay careful attention to the way in which international and domestic regulations can affect volunteerism in their country.

The following are examples of legal issues that affect volunteerism worldwide. Suggestions are offered on how laws could support an enabling environment for volunteerism.

1. Fundamental Rights and Freedoms

International and domestic laws on fundamental rights and freedoms protect volunteers and delimit the legal scope of voluntary activity, *inter alia*, when they provide for:

- the right to free assembly and peaceful association;
- the right not to be required to perform forced or compulsory labour;
- the right to participate actively in the political, economic, cultural, and social life of the country;
- the right to freedom of thought, conscience and religion;
- the right to a safe environment; and
- the right to promote human rights and fundamental freedoms.[1]

Volunteerism should be promoted within the context of these fundamental rights and freedoms. The law should prevent the term "volunteerism" from being misused, for example, to cover illegal forms of compulsory labour.

2. International Law

Many laws and regulations on international development cooperation and aid provide for volunteer participation through public and private institutions, agencies, and national and international organisations.[2] Though these laws encourage and in some way support volunteer participation in international missions and programmes, the protection afforded may not always suffice.

In the absence of any nationally and internationally recognised legal status for volunteers, they are often denied the strengthened diplomatic protection that is afforded under public international law to staffs of organisations for which they work.[3]

To avoid discouraging volunteer participation in international development cooperation and aid programmes run by intergovernmental, government and acknowledged non-governmental organisations whose non-voluntary staff enjoy such protection, governments and parliaments should demand that similar privileges and immunities extend to volunteers.

3. Labour Law

In the absence of a legally recognised status for volunteers and voluntary work, domestic labour law provisions affect volunteerism in many different ways.

The intention of some labour laws is to be inclusive. They expressly or tacitly extend the scope of their application to protect individuals other than paid employees.

The issue is whether such protection benefits volunteerism or whether it otherwise imposes unnecessary and undesirable burdens on volunteer users or the beneficiaries of volunteers' services. Unpaid voluntary work often shares very similar characteristics to paid work or employment: it is productive, valuable and contributes to the economy. Careful attention should therefore be paid to ensuring that labour law provisions do not discriminate against volunteers.

To avoid confusion between the concepts of employment and volunteerism, it may be necessary for some labour law provisions expressly to exclude volunteers from the scope of their application. For example, the general presumption that "work" is "paid work" should not apply to voluntary workers serving non-profit purposes. Volunteerism is non-paid, but it is not always cost-free.

The legal concept of "consideration for work" should not apply to any reasonable amounts volunteers may receive, such as reimbursements of out-of-pocket expenses related to their voluntary activities or the board or lodging they may be provided in the course of their work.

The law should clarify what kind of compensation volunteers may reasonably receive, according to their specific needs and service requirements, without being subjected to the general labour law system as "employees."[4]

Health and Safety

Provisions establishing the right to a healthy and safe environment at work are very often inclusive.

They require diligent and responsible behaviour on the part of employers with respect to all those who may be affected by their undertaking. These provisions actually guarantee some basic protection for volunteers without imposing any untenable burdens on volunteer-involving organisations.

Provisions on the right to a healthy and safe environment should be extended to cover volunteers at work.[5]

Liability of Volunteers

Volunteers should be protected in the event of damages or injuries they may cause in the course of their work.[6]

Labour laws should provide for the transfer of liability of volunteers to the private or public entities for which they work, as is the case for paid employees. When transferring liability from volunteers to non-profit volunteer-involving organisations, the law should encourage or prescribe the subscription of liability insurance policies to cover the risks.

Minimum Wage

When boundaries between the legal framework for employment and volunteerism are not clearly established by law, non-profit organisations often stop short of offering protection to volunteers for fear of having to offer volunteers the complete package of rights and duties corresponding to paid employees, including minimum wage provisions.

Volunteers should be expressly excluded from the application of minimum wage provisions.

Again, volunteers are not paid workers. The amounts volunteers may be offered in the form of reimbursement of reasonable expenses and the necessary subsistence support for the accomplishment of their assignments should not qualify as "consideration for work."[7]

Employee Volunteering

There is a growing interest in the private sector in promoting employee volunteering as an expression of corporate social responsibility. In some circumstances, for example, when an employer encourages staff to volunteer for a specific non-profit organisation with which the employer has a collaboration agreement, especially if this happens during working hours, the time spent can be considered as "hours worked," and thus fall under the frame-work of labour laws. In such cases, the employer is bound to pay the minimum wage, overtime premiums and other related provisions ensuring protection for employees.

Labour laws should encourage and facilitate employee volunteering. However, it is important that the law provide adequate protection for employees while avoiding the legal uncertainty that currently prevents many employers from encouraging participation of their staff in voluntary activity.[8]

> *Social welfare and health care are areas where volunteering has traditionally been very strong.*

The law can also encourage employee participation by allowing employees to take sabbatical time off from work to serve on a voluntary basis in non-profit organisations, without detriment to the contract with the employer.[9]

4. Tax Law

In some countries, any economic compensation is taxable as "personal income"—even reimbursement of travel expenses and allowances for food and lodging. This hinders the recruitment of volunteers from less favourable economic backgrounds.

To facilitate the recruitment of volunteers from all economic backgrounds, tax provisions should expressly exempt volunteers from paying taxes on the amounts they may receive as reimbursement of expenses or for subsistence support, provided that these amounts are "reasonable" and "necessary" for the purposes of their volunteer assignments.[10]

Furthermore, tax regulations can be strategically established to ensure sustainability of voluntary action, for example by:

- encouraging private, individual or corporate funding, through tax exemptions and deductions, to organisations utilising volunteers. The concept of donation should include the secondment of employees to work on a temporary or part-time basis;[11] and

- granting tax exemptions and benefits, including on income tax and other duties, such as property transfer tax, under certain conditions.[12]

5. Social Welfare Law

Social welfare and health care are areas where volunteering has traditionally been very strong. Although the State has ultimate responsibility in these sectors, in many countries citizen participation is considered to be of fundamental importance to help meet these needs.

Laws regulating social welfare and health-related work have a considerable impact on volunteerism, especially, though not only, in those countries where the bulk of social welfare work is carried out by volunteer-involving organisations.[13]

Social welfare laws which have an impact on the nature of volunteer engagement can directly influence social inclusion and integration of certain social groups, such as the elderly, or members of migrant or ethnic minorities.

In most countries with public social welfare and health-care schemes, volunteers do not enjoy special status *per se*, and they are therefore subject, as individuals, to the general rules concerning entitlements to state social welfare benefits. A volunteer's entitlement to public benefits in such cases will depend on whether the voluntary activity affects any parallel recognised legal status he or she may enjoy as a student, an unemployed person, or a person recognised as unfit for employment, which may involve entitlements.[14]

For example, individuals receiving unemployment benefits and who are required to look for a job on a full-time basis risk losing entitlements because volunteer work does not allow them to meet such a basic requirement. The law should address this situation, and for example, limit the time and conditions under which individuals in receipt of subsistence benefits can dedicate to volunteering without losing their entitlements.

If there are no clear rules regarding the amounts volunteers may receive as reimbursement of expenses or subsistence support related to their activities, then they also risk losing low-income support or family benefits, on the grounds that they are being remunerated for their services. The law should not penalise involvement in voluntary action by depriving volunteers and their families of social benefits they would otherwise receive. Such risks generally increase in cases where volunteers engage in full-time and long-term voluntary service programmes, especially if this occurs outside their countries of residence.

Social welfare laws should establish clear conditions under which benefit claimants are permitted to volunteer without losing their entitlements.

Furthermore, volunteers and the organisations in which they are involved should not generally be subjected to social and health scheme contributions, as this prevents less-resourced organisations from organising voluntary activities. To the extent possible, the funding of such protection should be assumed by the State.

6. Immigration Law

In the absence of a national and international legal definition of what constitutes voluntary activity, foreign citizens wishing to enter a given country for the purposes of volunteering, for example, through acknowledged international cooperation programmes, often encounter additional obstacles when applying for entry and residence permits. In many cases volunteers are issued inadequate visas and residence permits, such as tourist, student or business visas. This can be a considerable burden for the volunteer-involving organisations, and often means expatriate volunteers are unable to join their projects or to stay for the full duration of the volunteer assignment.

Immigration law should facilitate the entry of volunteers into a country for the purposes of participating in acknowledged international cooperation programmes or projects. This might include establishing clear legal conditions for the issuance of volunteer visas, or allowing work permits to be issued to foreign nationals who intend to undertake activities "of a charitable nature,"[15] or permitting inclusive provisions for the entry of specialised workers who can contribute to national economic and social development.[16]

7. Regulatory Frameworks for Non-profit or Charitable Organisations[17]

Non-profit or charitable organisations, including secular and religious associations and foundations, political parties and trade unions, represent some of the most appropriate arenas in which massive volunteerism can be developed and effectively managed. All of them involve citizens as volunteer-participants in their activities. Some are engaged in promoting volunteerism directly, managing volunteer efforts, building up worldwide networks of volunteers, raising awareness and lobbying for further recognition and support for voluntary action.

Creating an enabling legal environment for the establishment of non-governmental organisations is paramount to the further development of volunteerism.

National legislation should allow for the realisation of a strong civil society, in which networks of volunteers and volunteer-involving organisations across communities and nations will be able to improve upon their experiences and optimise their efforts.

This can be done by establishing an enabling legal framework for non-profit or charitable organisations that:

- encourages the establishment of both formal and informal (non-registered) volunteer organisations;
- recognises their independence from the State and from the business sector;
- improves their visibility and credibility, including through the establishment of reasonable conditions for their official registration, with a view to setting adequate standards of governance, accountability and transparency in the carrying out of their functions;
- ensures sustainability of the sector by mandating the State to support and facilitate their activities, including by assisting organisations in finding ways of securing benefits, for example through tax incentives and other funding opportunities;

- establishes mechanisms for dialogue between the State and the non-profit sector; and
- ensures the coordination of the implementation of applicable State policies and measures to promote, support and enhance the capacity of non-profit organisations.

B. *Establishing a Legal Framework for Volunteerism*

In the absence of a clear definition of volunteerism or voluntary activity, some countries try to offer protection to volunteers by legally assimilating them with other categories, such as "employees." This has both positive and negative implications for the development of volunteerism. Unscrupulous employers must be prevented from abusively profiting from the undefined situation of the voluntary sector by using it to exploit cheap labour.

The need for laws concerning volunteers has generally been construed in terms of offering basic protection to volunteers outside of an existing legal framework for paid work or employment. That framework has been identified as unsuitable for the development of volunteerism.

In order for all countries to benefit fully from volunteerism and from the exchange of volunteers among countries, States should recognise volunteers as a legal category *per se*. This recognition should be in full alignment with the objectives of the International Year of Volunteers, 2001, endorsed by the United Nations General Assembly. These objectives address the promotion, recognition, facilitation and networking of volunteerism.

In other words, States and their legislatures should take appropriate steps to facilitate voluntary action and promote its development, while respecting the philosophy and capacity of all people, irrespective of background, to participate in voluntary activity.

Any law relevant to volunteers should enhance recognition of voluntary activity and remove any legal and regulatory barriers, and should certainly not create additional obstacles for engagement.

In both industrialised and developing countries, recent legislation on volunteerism has taken various forms including:

- laws encompassing and giving full recognition to the whole range of existing and potential expressions of voluntary activity in a democratic country, also referred to as framework laws on volunteerism;[18]
- laws and regulations supporting organised voluntary action and providing legal protection to volunteers acting through public or private organisations;[19] and
- laws and regulations promoting and supporting voluntary participation by specific groups, such as youth or unemployed persons, or promoting volunteerism in areas of special interest, such as social development work, international development

cooperation, fire brigades, civil protection[20] or disaster management.[21]

These laws and accompanying policy measures include important issues affecting volunteerism, such as legal recognition and acknowledgement, the definition and principles of voluntary activity, the legal status of volunteers, and the basic rules governing the relationship between volunteers and the organisations in which they are involved.

A single encompassing framework law for all types of voluntary action may, in many instances, facilitate the factoring of volunteerism into policy-making processes, and thus promote volunteering. Such a framework law could include models for use in purpose-specific legislation.

The main benefit of a framework law on volunteerism is that it can serve as a general legislative reference for further deepening and fine tuning the legal system in favour of voluntary action. Framework laws enhance recognition of the contributions of all individuals and groups volunteering for the common good, independent of their social background and area of activity.

There are some common elements within existing framework laws on volunteerism in the countries which have adopted them. These include the legal definition of a volunteer and voluntary activity as a concept distinct from employment, general principles of volunteerism, codes of conduct that determine the relationship between volunteers and the organisations in which they are involved, and measures to further recognise, facilitate and promote the development of volunteerism and networking of volunteers. Different issues are analysed below and some considerations to be taken into account in the relevant legislative processes are highlighted.

1. Legal Definitions

There is no universal model for a legal definition of the terms "volunteer" and "volunteerism." Different national laws and regulations establish different definitions, depending on traditions and culture. Sometimes, the absolute need for volunteer support leads to different definitions being used within a single country, depending on the circumstances.

When considering the wording of these definitions, legislators should take care not to disregard the potential benefits of all existing kinds of voluntary activity. It is of paramount importance that a framework law on volunteerism provide the most comprehensive and flexible definitions possible for volunteers and voluntary activity. For example:

- "Volunteerism is the group of activities carried out by individuals, associations or legal entities, for the common good, by free choice and without the intention of financial gain, outside the framework of any employment, mercantile or civil service relationship"; or

- "A volunteer is an individual who, by free choice, offers his or her time, work and skills, occasionally or on a regular basis, without expectation of compensation, other than reimbursement of reasonable expenses and subsistence allowance necessary for the accomplishment of his or her assignments as a volunteer, for the public benefit, individually or within the framework of informal or officially registered non-governmental non-profit organisations or national or international public entities."

These definitions include the participation of all men and women, who freely offer their time, work and skills, rather than goods, money or facilities, without compulsion or coercion of any kind or by law. They may do so either occasionally or on a regular basis, according to an agreement for cooperation with an officially acknowledged or informal organisation, for the common good, not only for their private interests, in their home countries or abroad. The volunteer does not work for financial gain, although he or she may receive reasonable compensation and necessary support for the accomplishment of his or her assignment as a volunteer.

The legal definitions of volunteers and voluntary activity should allow for a clear distinction between what constitutes voluntary unpaid work and paid employment. Volunteers require legal treatment and protection distinguishable from that applicable to "paid workers." This is necessary to protect volunteers and the organisations in which they are involved from the potentially pernicious application of certain labour, social welfare and tax law provisions, as mentioned above. In this regard, the most important issue relates to the absence of financial reward for voluntary activity.

The law should begin with the assumption that volunteers are not paid for their services. Volunteers are not motivated by financial gain. Reimbursement of reasonable expenses or the provision of necessary subsistence support for volunteers (in money or in kind, in the form of food, accommodation and pocket money) must be assessed, taking into account that volunteering incurs costs and that ideally all citizens, independent of their financial resources, should be in a position to volunteer if they so desire.

Several considerations are relevant to the assessment of whether or not any reimbursement of expenses or subsistence support is reasonable or necessary for the effective accomplishment of the voluntary activity. These include whether the individual has any reasonable expectation of compensation either at present or in the future.

2. General Principles of Volunteerism

In order to further delimit and clarify the essential elements of voluntary activity, laws should foresee a set of general principles governing the development of volunteerism.[22] Principles of volunteerism may vary significantly from country to country. Generally they include many of the following basic standards:

- volunteers participate on the basis of freely-expressed consent;
- volunteering is not compulsorily undertaken in order to receive pensions or government allowances;
- volunteering is not carried out in expectation of any financial gain;
- volunteering complements, but must not result in, the downsizing or replacement of paid employment;
- volunteerism should be encouraged with a certain degree of autonomy from the public authorities, to safeguard its independence;
- volunteering is a legitimate way in which citizens can participate actively in the development of community and social life and address human needs;
- volunteers act for the common good and on the basis of a social commitment;
- volunteering promotes human rights and equality;
- volunteerism respects the rights, dignity and culture of the communities involved;
- volunteer recruitment is based on equal opportunity and nondiscrimination;
- volunteering is inspired by democratic, pluralistic, participative and caring social tenets.

3. The Relationship Between Volunteers and Volunteer-Involving Organisations

Some framework laws on volunteering include provisions governing relationships between volunteers and the organisations in which they work. This can further help to clarify the borders between volunteerism and employment, encourage a responsible commitment on the part of the different protagonists, and protect volunteers.

The challenge is to establish practical rules which take into careful consideration the social and economic reality of the country and which permit volunteers and volunteer-involving organisations to develop their activities flexibly, according to capacities and needs.

A code of conduct for volunteers and volunteer-involving organisations could include the following provisions:[23]

Protection of Volunteers:

- The right to receive the necessary information, training, supervision, personal and technical support for the discharge of their duties;
- Insurance against the risk of accidents and illness related to the volunteer activity;

- The right to work in safe, secure and healthy conditions;
- The right to be reimbursed for reasonable expenses related to the volunteer activity, as well as to be provided with basic subsistence support for food and accommodation whenever the volunteer assignment so requires, and previously agreed with the host organisation; and
- Appropriate accreditation, describing the nature and length of time of the volunteer activity, as well as certification acknowledging the volunteer's contribution at the end of the service;

Duties of Volunteers:
- To respect the objectives and observe the regulations of the organisation in which they are involved;
- To respect the rights, beliefs and opinions of beneficiaries; and
- To participate in any necessary training courses provided by the host organisation.

Responsibilities of Volunteer-Involving Organisations:
- To ensure that an appropriate insurance policy is in place for volunteers, covering eventual risks of accident or illness directly related to the volunteer activity;
- To reimburse any expenses incurred by volunteers in fulfilling their volunteer tasks, up to the reasonable limits previously agreed with the volunteer;
- To provide volunteers with appropriate infrastructure for the discharge of their duties;
- To provide appropriate information to their volunteers on the nature and condition of their voluntary assignment;
- To provide volunteers with appropriate training;
- To ensure safe, secure and healthy conditions at work, in accordance with the nature of the volunteer activity;
- To provide their volunteers with accreditation and issue a certificate acknowledging their contribution at the end of their service; and
- To assume third-party liability for any damages or injuries their volunteers may cause by any action or omission in the course their voluntary work, provided that the volunteers act with due diligence and in good faith.

4. Recognition of Volunteer Contributions

Laws on volunteering should contribute to enhancing recognition of the contributions of volunteers. Examples include:
- encouraging volunteer-involving organisations to issue volunteer certificates attesting to their contributions;

- acknowledging the educational value of volunteerism though a system of academic credits;[24] and
- counting the time spent on voluntary activity for the purposes of future social welfare pensions, when applicable.[25]

5. The Role of Governments

The extent to which laws contribute to promoting volunteerism is strongly determined by the set of policy measures in place to implement those laws. Such policy measures often include:[26]

- awareness campaigns on the values and benefits of volunteerism;
- technical, logistical and financial assistance for organisations which involve volunteers, including training and information services;
- financial support measures for volunteers, such as reductions for public transport;
- inclusion of volunteers in public social welfare and health-care schemes when their voluntary activity prevents other forms of coverage; and
- development and support for research on volunteerism, including the establishment of national mechanisms to measure the contribution of volunteerism to human development.

Governments should also examine the possibility of supporting national and local volunteer committees with broad representational participation. Such supports should also involve relevant public authorities and private actors, including decision makers, public and private volunteer organisations, business and other important donors, and academia.[27] Such institutions can also contribute to monitoring the implementation of laws and identifying additional issues to be taken up in future legislation. They are also useful forums in which to identify the roles of the different protagonists, better coordinate their activities, exchange best practices, and identify possible areas for cooperation, including mobilising human and financial resources.

6. The Role of Members of Parliament

In most cases relating to the maintenance of an enabling environment for voluntary action, parliamentarians will be considering legislation on issues which do not concern volunteers directly, but where volunteer support is vital to the success of the action proposed. Parliamentarians may wish to establish consultative systems to draw attention to such issues, so that they can underscore the cross-cutting nature and contribution of voluntary action to a country's well-being. They can advocate for supportive, pro-volunteering policies, laws and budgetary allocations. Through this, they can mobilise action in favour of volunteerism by influencing governments and public officials, including by promoting the establishment of parliamentary and public forums for debate on the issues. In many cases this will link naturally to their representative function in the parliament and their own wish to represent community issues positively.

IV. Conclusions and Recommendations

Legislation has a considerable impact on volunteerism, and indeed, can be a significant determinant of the extent to which it flourishes. The issues raised and discussed in this Note reflect some of the most evident expressions of the impact that laws can have on volunteerism. While some laws protect and facilitate the engagement of volunteers, others have the opposite effect, usually unintentionally.

For the benefits of volunteerism to be fully realised in each country's context, the following steps may be considered:

- establish a parliamentary committee or a similar group to address issues pertaining to volunteerism and to consider and develop specific policy strategies and measures to improve the framework conditions for national and international volunteer action;
- ensure that the contribution of volunteers to economic and social development is recognised and protected in all legislation and other government action relevant to the sector in question;
- intensify awareness-raising activities, for example, through supporting and promoting International Volunteer Day, 5 December, and other significant days and events in which volunteerism is a significant component;
- host activities aimed at supporting and giving recognition to the efforts of volunteers;
- maintain close consultation with volunteer-involving organisations as well as other stakeholders, such as the private sector, academia and the media, including through public hearings, accessible to the volunteers themselves;
- support the creation and functioning of national and regional volunteer centres or even volunteer development agencies as permanent structures allowing for continuous dialogue between policy-makers and legislators on the one hand and the principle stakeholders in volunteer action on the other;
- approve budget lines for the support of pro-volunteer actions;
- exchange information and practice;
- develop, support and facilitate research on the contribution of volunteerism to social development and the impact of national legislation on volunteerism from both a national and an international comparative perspective;[28]

- include references to volunteerism in state of the nation addresses;
- integrate volunteerism in its various forms and as a mainstreamed issue in national policies, programmes and reports, for example factoring volunteer contributions into national and international strategic goals; such as reports on the Millennium Development Goals; and
- ensure that international, regional and national policy and legislation do not impose obstacles that reduce the capacity of citizens to engage in voluntary action, ensuring diversity and flexibility of all potential expressions of volunteerism.

As States strive to achieve the Millennium Development Goals, volunteerism offers enormous resources. States should harness that potential, in part by ensuring that national laws foster, rather than deter, volunteerism. Six billion people have something to contribute toward the Millennium Development Goals, and parliamentarians have a vital role to play, especially by:

- removing existing barriers in laws and regulations;
- mainstreaming volunteerism in legislative processes; and
- enhancing opportunities for volunteering, through the creation of appropriate volunteer legislation in partnership with all stakeholders.

Endnotes

1. United Nations General Assembly Resolution 53/144 of 8 March 1999, adopting the Declaration on the Right and Responsibility of Individuals, Groups and Organs of Society to Promote Universally Recognised Human Rights and Fundamental Freedoms (Article 1 of the Declaration).
2. Lebanon-Italy: Development Cooperation Agreement between the Government of the Italian Republic and the Government of the Republic of Lebanon.
3. Convention on the Privileges and Immunities of the United Nations of 13 February 1946, Convention on the Privileges and Immunities of the Specialized Agencies of 21 November 1947, Convention on the Safety of United Nations and Associated Personnel of 9 December 1994; see also the Geneva Conventions of 12 August 1949.
4. United States (Federal): Fair Labor Standards Act (FLSA).
5. South Africa: Occupational Health and Safety Act, No. 85, of 1993; United Kingdom: Health and Safety at Work Act of 1974 (Section 3); New Zealand: Health and Safety in Employment Amendment Act of 2002.
6. Canada (Nova Scotia): Volunteer Protection Act, S.N.S. 2002; c. 14 (available at: http://www.gov.ns.ca/legi/legc/bills/58th_2nd/3rd_read/b098.htm); Australia: Volunteers (Protection from Liability) Act of 2002; United States: Volunteer Protection Act of 1997.
7. United Kingdom: Case law: *Chaudri v. Migrant Advisory Service (MAS)*, 1997; source: *Legal Status of Volunteers in Europe*, 2003, Association of Voluntary Service Organisations (AVSO) and European Volunteer Centre-Centre Européen du Volontariat (CEV) joint research study, available at: http://www.avso.org/en/activities/CEV&AVSO.htm and http://www.cev.be/legal_status.htm.

Historical Overview of National Service 57

8. United States (Federal): Fair Labor Standards Act (FLSA).
9. Belgium: Source: *European Union without Compulsory Military Service: Consequences for Alternative Service—A comparative study on the policies in EU member states*, 2002, Gerd Greune and Michaela Lai, European Bureau for Conscientious Objectors (EBCO), EU-Study Papers, Heinrich Böll Foundation, Brussels office.
10. Canada: Income Tax Act (ITA); Belgium: Internal Administrative Regulation, *Circulaire*, G. Rh. 241/509.803 of 5 March 1999.
11. Mozambique: Decree No. 21/2002 of 30 June 2002

    United Kingdom: Inland Revenue, http://www.inlandrevenue.gov.uk/pdfs/ir64.pdf; Case Law: *Chaudri v. Migrant Advisory Service (MAS)*, 1997; source: *Legal Status of Volunteers in Europe*, 2003, Association of Voluntary Service Organisations (AVSO) and European Volunteer Centre-Centre Européen du Volontariat (CEV) joint research study (available at: http://www.avso.org/en/activities/CEV&AVSO.htm and http://www.cev.be/legal_status.htm).
12. Mozambique: Right to Free Association Act No. 8/91 of 18 July 1991; Associations of Public Benefit Decree No. 37/2000 of 17 October 2000; Non-Governmental Non-Profit Organisations Decree No. 21/2002.
13. South Africa: National Welfare Amendment Act, No. 77 of 1978 and White Paper for Social Welfare of 1997.
14. The Netherlands: Subsistence Benefits Act, source: *Legal Status of Volunteers in Europe*, 2003, Association of Voluntary Service Organisations (AVSO) and European Volunteer Centre-Centre Européen du Volontariat (CEV) joint research study (available at: http://www.avso.org/en/ activities/CEV&AVSO.htm and http://www.cev.be/legal_status.htm).
15. Canada (Federal): Immigration and Refugee Protection Act (Section 205); South Africa: Immigration Act, No. 13 of 2002 (Section 11); Brazil: Temporary Visa Regulations.
16. Uruguay: Decree on the Entry and Stay of Foreign Citizens in the Territory of the Eastern Republic of Uruguay.
17. Examples of laws encouraging the establishment of non-governmental organisations across the world:

    Albania: Act No. 8781 of 3 May 2001 amending Act No. 7580 of 29 July 1994; Civil Code of the Republic of Albania; Non-Profit Organisations Act, No. 8788 of 7 May 2001; and Registration of Non-Profit Organisations Act, No. 8789 of 7 May 2001.

    Sri Lanka: Voluntary Social Services Organisations (Registration and Supervision) Act, No. 31 of 1980, as amended by Act No. 8 of 1998.

    South Africa: Non-Profit Organisations Act, No. 71 of 1997. The Act states that within the limits prescribed by law, every organ of State must determine and coordinate the implementation of its policies and measures in a manner designed to promote, support and enhance the capacity of non-profit organisations to perform their functions.

    Russian Federation (Federal): Charitable Activities and Charitable Organisations Act.

    Japan: Law to Promote Specified Non-Profit Activities of 25 March 1998 (Chapter I, Article 2).
18. Examples of framework laws on volunteerism:

    Colombia: Act No. 720 of 29 December 2001, on volunteerism.

    Brazil: Act No. 9608 of 18 February 1998, on volunteerism.
19. Examples of laws and regulations supporting organised voluntary action and providing certain legal protection to volunteers acting through public or private organisations:

- Laws establishing a general framework for the development of volunteerism within non-governmental non-profit organisations or public entities:

    Spain: Act No. 6/1996 of 15 January 1996, on volunteerism.

    Italy: Act No. 266/1991 on volunteering.

- Laws limiting the liability of volunteers working in organisations:

    Canada (Nova Scotia): Volunteer Protection Act of 2002.

    Australia (South Australia): Volunteers Protection Act, No. 65 of 2001.

    United States (Federal): Volunteer Protection Act of 1997.

20. Tunisia: Decree 99-2428 of 1 November 1999, establishing the methods and procedures for the use of civil volunteers by the national office of civil protection.

21. Examples of laws and regulations promoting voluntary participation of specific target groups or in areas of special interest:

    Senegal: National (Youth) Civic Service Act, No. 98-25 of 7 April 1998.

    Italy: National (Youth) Civic Service Act, No. 64/2001 of 6 March 2001; Cooperation to Development Voluntary Service Act, No. 49/1987; Promotion of Social Organisations Act, No. 383/2000.

    Czech Republic: (Youth) Volunteerism Act of 2002.

    Germany (Federal): Promotion of a Voluntary Year of Social Service (for Youth) Act of 1964, and Promotion of a Voluntary Year of Ecological Service (for Youth) Act of 1993, as amended.

    Japan: Promotion of Specified Non-profit Activities Act of 25 March 1998.

    Portugal: Regulation of the *Lusíadas* Programme, Ministerial Order No. 745 - H/96 of 18 December 1996.

    Tunisia: Act No. 93-121 of 27 December 1993, establishing the National Office of Civil Protection.

    South Africa: Maritime and Aeronautical Search and Rescue Act, No. 44 of 2002, Disasters Management Act, No. 57 of 2002.

    Albania: Act No. 8765 of 26 March 2001, on civil emergencies.

22. Colombia: Act No. 720 of 29 December 2001, on volunteerism.

    Portugal: Act No. 71/98 of 3 November 1998, on volunteerism.

23. Brazil: Act No. 9608 of 18 February 1998, on volunteerism.

    Spain: Act No. 6/1996 of 15 January 1996, on volunteerism.

    Italy: Act No. 266/1991 on volunteering.

    Colombia: Act No. 720 of 29 December 2001, on volunteerism.

    Portugal: Act No. 71/98 of 3 November 1998, on volunteerism.

24. Italy: National (Youth) Civic Service Act, No. 64/2001 of 6 March 2001.

25. Senegal: National (Youth) Civic Service Act, No. 98-25 of 7 April 1998; Italy: National (Youth) Civic Service Act, No. 64/2001 of 6 March 2001.

26. Portugal: Act No. 71/98 of 3 November 1998, on volunteerism.

    Czech Republic: (Youth) Volunteerism Act of 2002.

    Senegal: National (Youth) Civic Service Act, No. 98-25 of 7 April 1998.

27. Portugal: Resolution No. 50/2000, establishing the Permanent National Volunteerism Council.

    Colombia: Act No. 720 of 29 December 2001, on volunteerism.

28. Examples of country-focus studies and comparative research on legislation affecting volunteers:

    - *Legal Status of Volunteers in Europe*, 2003, Association of Voluntary Service Organisations (AVSO) and European Volunteer Centre-Centre Européen du

Volontariat (CEV) joint research study (available at: http://www.avso.org/en/activities/CEV&AVSO.htm and http://www.cev.be/legal_status.htm).
- *Situación Legal del Voluntariado en Iberoamerica—Estudio Comparado*, Organización Iberoamericana de Juventud (OIJ) (available at: http://www.oij.org/voluntariadooij.pdf).

II. Military Service and Conscription

Editor's Introduction

Many Americans equate the words "national service" with military service, and despite reassurances by the government, many fear the possibility of a draft. With recruitment falling below target numbers and with the country involved in prolonged conflicts in both Afghanistan and Iraq, rumors are surfacing that the United States may be forced to reinstate conscription. Indeed, in January 2003, Representative Charles Rangel of New York introduced legislation to bring back the draft. An opponent of the invasion of Iraq, which was then still in its planning stages, Rangel felt that Americans would be less likely to support the war if they thought that they or their children might have to fight it. The bill never had much chance of passing, however, and was quietly defeated in a vote of 402–2, with even Rangel voting against it. Nevertheless, a year later, during the 2004 presidential election, rumors continued to swirl, especially on the Internet, that a draft was likely, despite both candidates' unambiguous denials.

Responding to such conjecture, Secretary of Defense Donald H. Rumsfeld wrote "Rumors About a Draft Are False," in which he stated "To my knowledge . . . the idea of reinstating [the] draft has never been debated, endorsed, discussed, theorized, pondered or even whispered by anyone in the Bush administration." Rumsfeld claimed that conscription would create more problems than it would solve, commenting, "I know the inequities and the problems—for both our society and our military—associated with compelling people to serve against their will in the armed forces."

Rangel's call for a draft, however, was motivated by the disparities he and others perceive in the current all-volunteer military. In his article "Bring Back the Draft," he wrote, "A disproportionate number of the poor and members of minority groups make up the enlisted ranks of the military, while the most privileged Americans are underrepresented or absent."

Phillip Carter and Paul Glastris, in "The Case for the Draft," rely on issues of pragmatism and practicality rather than social justice in their argument in favor of conscription. Asserting that the U.S. does not have sufficient forces to sustain the current missions in Iraq and Afghanistan, the authors outline a series of five options to address the problem absent a draft, none of which they consider feasible. Consequently, the only viable alternative, they conclude, is for the government to "impose a requirement that no four-year college or university be allowed to accept a student, male or female, unless and until that student had completed a 12-month to two-year term of service." Their proposal, like Rangel's, includes a provision allowing draftees to opt for non-military service in programs like AmeriCorps or the Peace Corps.

Richard A. Posner, in "An Army of the Willing," presents perhaps the most fundamental argument against conscription, describing it as a violation of personal liberty and free will. Posner equates a draft with slavery, "in the sense that a conscript is a person deprived of the ownership of his own labor; and slavery is the ultimate commodification, because it treats a human being as a salable good. . . . Surely it is conscription that treats the persons conscripted as if the state does own them."

In "Schroder to End Conscription in Push for EU Rapid Reaction Force," Tony Paterson discusses efforts to abolish military conscription in Germany, which he describes as a "historic milestone." While the United States drafted its last soldier in 1973, until recently much of Europe had maintained a policy of conscription. In the past decade, however, France, Austria, Greece, and Spain have all shifted in whole or in part toward a volunteer military. Paterson also describes French and German efforts to establish a pan-European military force that would "act as a counterweight to America's global military dominance."

Rumors About a Draft Are False

By Donald H. Rumsfeld
U.S. Department of Defense (*www.defenselink.mil*), October 28, 2004

The peculiar thing about myths is that even the most far-fetched can be nearly impossible to extinguish. This is especially so when there is a vested interest in some quarters in keeping them alive. Like many Americans, I have recently heard a great deal of misinformed talk about a so-called "secret plan" to bring back the draft. This plot is so secret that it doesn't exist. Neither our commander in chief nor the secretary of defense know anything about it. That's because it simply is not true.

Let me be even more emphatic on that point. To my knowledge, in the time I have served as secretary of defense, the idea of reinstating draft has never been debated, endorsed, discussed, theorized, pondered or even whispered by anyone in the Bush administration. When asked about it, the president has flatly rejected the idea. Similarly, the chairman of the Joint Chiefs of Staff has said a draft is not needed or desirable. And the U.S. House of Representatives voted down a bill, offered by several Democratic congressmen, to reinstate the draft by a resounding 402–2 just two weeks ago. Yet based on absolutely no actual evidence, partisans, conspiracy mongers and troublemakers are attempting to scare and mislead young Americans by insisting that a draft is coming. This is mischiefmaking masquerading as a serious policy debate. It is shameful.

This entire deceit is underhanded and just plain wrong. Unfortunately, regrettably, inexcusably, thanks to the available transmission belt in the media, it seems to be working. One recent opinion poll suggests that about half of America's young people surveyed believe that President Bush favors reinstating the draft. I take this issue seriously and personally. As a member of Congress in the 1960s, I was one of the first to support an all-volunteer force.

I know the inequities and the problems—for both our society and our military—associated with compelling people to serve against their will in the armed forces.

Quite beyond the draft's inequities and inefficiencies, the United States simply does not need a draft. America has about 295 million people and some 2.6 million serving in the active and reserve components of our military. We don't need compulsion to attract and retain the people we need to serve our country. As it stands today,

---

Article by Donald H. Rumsfeld. Courtesy of DefenseLINK.

the active Army and Marine Corps continue to exceed their recruiting goals despite the high pace of activity. Retention is also doing well. Particularly striking are re-enlistment rates for units that have deployed overseas. Of the Army's 10 active duty divisions, nine are exceeding re-enlistment goals by 5 percent or more. The United States is so fortunate that every day so many brave and talented young men and women willingly sign up to serve their country, knowing full well—just from watching the nightly news—the dangers and sacrifices involved. Each one is a volunteer, and if it happened that we were to not have enough people to serve, all we would have to do is what any other organization would do—and that is increase the incentives and make military service a more attractive option for the best and brightest young people. There is stress on our forces—but not because of any shortage of uniformed personnel.

For example, there are over 1 million soldiers in the active Army, Army Reserve and National Guard. Of those, less than 12 percent are actually deployed to the Iraq and Afghanistan theaters. And the Army has already increased its active strength by as many as 30,000 troops since Sept. 11, 2001. The issue is that our forces, particularly the Army, are not properly organized for the post–Cold War era. Too many skills needed on active duty are heavily concentrated in the Reserve components.

Too many of the active forces are not readily deployable. Too many military personnel—tens of thousands—are performing tasks that could and should be performed by civilians.

We have undertaken a range of initiatives to increase the pool of deployable troops within the armed forces and the quality of life for service members and their families. The result will be that individual troops will be deployed less often, for shorter periods of time and with more predictability. With a professional, all-volunteer force, the U.S. military won the Cold War, liberated Afghanistan and Iraq, and has kept the peace in Asia and Europe. And the all-volunteer force will win the global war on terror.

Bring Back the Draft

By Charles B. Rangel
The New York Times, December 31, 2002

President Bush and his administration have declared a war against terrorism that may soon involve sending thousands of American troops into combat in Iraq. I voted against the Congressional resolution giving the president authority to carry out this war—an engagement that would dwarf our military efforts to find Osama bin Laden and bring him to justice.

But as a combat veteran of the Korean conflict, I believe that if we are going to send our children to war, the governing principle must be that of shared sacrifice. Throughout much of our history, Americans have been asked to shoulder the burden of war equally.

That's why I will ask Congress next week to consider and support legislation I will introduce to resume the military draft.

Carrying out the administration's policy toward Iraq will require long-term sacrifices by the American people, particularly those who have sons and daughters in the military. Yet the Congress that voted overwhelmingly to allow the use of force in Iraq includes only one member who has a child in the enlisted ranks of the military—just a few more have children who are officers.

I believe that if those calling for war knew that their children were likely to be required to serve—and to be placed in harm's way—there would be more caution and a greater willingness to work with the international community in dealing with Iraq. A renewed draft will help bring a greater appreciation of the consequences of decisions to go to war.

Service in our nation's armed forces is no longer a common experience. A disproportionate number of the poor and members of minority groups make up the enlisted ranks of the military, while the most privileged Americans are underrepresented or absent.

We need to return to the tradition of the citizen soldier—with alternative national service required for those who cannot serve because of physical limitations or reasons of conscience.

There is no doubt that going to war against Iraq will severely strain military resources already burdened by a growing number of obligations. There are daunting challenges facing the 1.4 million men and women in active military service and those in our National Guard and Reserve. The Pentagon has said that up to 250,000 troops may be mobilized for the invasion of Iraq. An addi-

---

Copyright © 2002 by The New York Times Co. Reprinted with permission.

tional 265,000 members of the National Guard and Reserve, roughly as many as were called up during the Persian Gulf War in 1991, may also be activated.

Already, we have long-term troop commitments in Europe and the Pacific, with an estimated 116,000 troops in Europe, 90,000 in the Pacific (nearly 40,000 in Japan and 38,000 in Korea) and additional troop commitments to operations in Afghanistan, Bosnia, Kosovo and elsewhere. There are also military trainers in countries across the world, including the Philippines, Colombia and Yemen.

We can expect the evolving global war on terrorism to drain our military resources even more, stretching them to the limit.

The administration has yet to address the question of whether our military is of sufficient strength and size to meet present and future commitments. Those who would lead us into war have the obligation to support an all-out mobilization of Americans for the war effort, including mandatory national service that asks something of us all.

The Case for the Draft

BY PHILLIP CARTER AND PAUL GLASTRIS
THE WASHINGTON MONTHLY, MARCH 2005

The United States has occupied many foreign lands over the last half century—Germany and Japan in World War II, and, on a much smaller scale, Haiti, Bosnia, and Kosovo in the 1990s. In all these cases, we sponsored elections and handed-off to democratic governments control of countries that were relatively stable, secure, and reasonably peaceful.

In Iraq, we failed to do this, despite heroic efforts by U.S. and coalition troops. The newly-elected Iraqi government inherits a country in which assassinations, kidnappings, suicide bombings, pipeline sabotages, and beheadings of foreigners are daily occurrences. For the last eight months, the ranks of the insurgency have been growing faster than those of the security forces of the provisional Iraqi government—and an alarming number of those government forces are secretly working for the insurgency. American-led combat operations in Ramadi and Fallujah killed large numbers of the enemy; but at the price of fanning the flames of anti-American hatred and dispersing the insurrection throughout Iraq. Despite nearly two years of effort, American troops and civilian administrators have failed to restore basic services to much of the central part of the country where a majority of Iraqis live. The U.S. military has not even been able to secure the 7-mile stretch of highway leading from the Baghdad airport to the Green Zone where America's own embassy and the seat of the Iraqi government are headquartered.

How we got to this point is by now quite obvious. Even many of the war's strongest supporters admit that the Bush administration grievously miscalculated by invading Iraq with too few troops and then by stubbornly refusing to augment troop numbers as the country descended into violent mayhem after the fall of Saddam.

This analysis, of course, presumes that it was ever possible to invade and quickly pacify Iraq, given the country's religious-ethnic divisions and history of tyranny. But it also presumes that the fault is primarily one of judgment: that the president and key senior military officials made a mistake by accepting Defense Secretary Donald Rumsfeld's theory that a "transformed" American military can prevail in war without great masses of ground troops.

Reprinted with permission from *The Washington Monthly*. Copyright by Washington Monthly Publishing, LLC, 1319 F St. NW, Suite 710, Washington, DC 20004. (202) 393-5155. Web site: www.washingtonmonthly.com.

That judgment was indeed foolish; events have shown that, while a relatively modest American force can win a stunning battlefield victory; such a force is not enough to secure the peace.

But there's a deeper problem, one that any president who chose to invade a country the size of Iraq would have faced. In short, America's all-volunteer military simply cannot deploy and sustain enough troops to succeed in places like Iraq while still deterring threats elsewhere in the world. Simply adding more soldiers to the active duty force, as some in Washington are now suggesting, may sound like a good solution. But it's not, for sound operational and pragmatic reasons. America doesn't need a bigger standing army; it needs a deep bench of trained soldiers held in reserve who can be mobilized to handle the unpredictable but inevitable wars and humanitarian interventions of the future. And while there are several ways the all-volunteer force can create some extra surge capacity, all of them are limited.

The only effective solution to the manpower crunch is the one America has turned to again and again in its history: the draft. Not

> ***America's all-volunteer military simply cannot deploy and sustain enough troops to succeed in places like Iraq while still deterring threats elsewhere in the world.***

the mass combat mobilizations of World War II, nor the inequitable conscription of Vietnam—for just as threats change and war-fighting advances, so too must the draft. A modernized draft would demand that the privileged participate. It would give all who serve a choice over how they serve. And it would provide the military, on a "just in time" basis, large numbers of deployable ground troops, particularly the peacekeepers we'll need to meet the security challenges of the 21st century.

America has a choice. It can be the world's superpower, or it can maintain the current all-volunteer military, but it probably can't do both.

Plowing a Field with a Ferrari

Before the invasion of Iraq, Army Chief of Staff Eric Shinseki and Army Secretary Thomas White advised Rumsfeld that many more troops would be needed to secure Iraq (something on the order of 250,000 to 300,000). Secretary of State Colin Powell, whose State Department was shut out of the post-war planning process, also privately argued for a bigger force. A RAND Corporation analysis, published in summer 2003, offered a range of estimates for what size force would be necessary in Iraq. Using troops-to-population ratios from previous occupations, RAND projected that, two years after the invasion, it would take anywhere from 258,000 troops (the Bosnia model), to 321,000 (post–World War II Germany), to 526,000 (Kosovo) to secure the peace.

None of these figures seems, at first glance, unachievable for a U.S. military comprised of 1.4 million active-duty troops, 870,900 reservists, and 110,000 individual ready reservists (soldiers who have served their tour of duty and are not training with the reserves but who can by statute still be called up for service). And yet an Iraq deployment that has never exceeded 153,000 ground personnel has put so much stress on the military that a senior Army Reserve official has candidly stated that current rotation policies will lead to a "broken force." How can that be?

To answer that question, begin by deducting virtually the entire Navy and Air Force from the head count; the Iraq occupation has been almost exclusively a ground game, hence an Army and Marine operation. Next, consider that the United States sends into combat not individual soldiers but units, complete with unit equipment sets, unit leaders, and an organizational structure that facilitates command, control, and logistical support. So instead of counting individual soldiers—a meaningless exercise—one must look at how many *units* the United States could theoretically put on the ground if it wanted to mobilize every active and reserve soldier available. And if you do that, you come to a figure of roughly 600,000 troops. That's the total number of deployable soldiers that the United States could theoretically have called upon to man the initial invasion.

In practice, however, the Pentagon would never have sent that many troops to Iraq, for good reasons: It would have left the defense cupboard bare and served as an open invitation to America's enemies to make trouble elsewhere in the world. Massing a 600,000 force would have meant not only pulling nearly all frontline troops out of Korea, but also mobilizing the poorly-resourced divisions of the National Guard, the third-string crew that the president can call on when the first string (active troops) and the second string (the Guard's elite "enhanced" reserve brigades) are depleted.

Given the need to hold troops in reserve for deterrence purposes, the Pentagon had perhaps 400,000 troops available for the invasion. Yet that number includes many troops in specialized fields that are of little or no use in desert warfare or peacekeeping—offloading equipment in sea ports, for instance. Such troops could have been reshaped into provisional infantry units, as the Army has done with artillery and air-defense formations, but that would've taken time. The number of troops with units that would actually have been of use in Iraq was probably closer to the figures that Gen. Shinseki and Secretary White have suggested: 250,000 to 300,000—in other words, the lower end of what RAND estimated would be required for success.

But even that number is deceptive. It is the size of the force that could have been initially sent into Iraq, not the number that could have realistically been *sustained* there. Because so many soldiers in the all-volunteer military are married with families (compared to conscript armies), and because soldiers must periodically be induced or persuaded to voluntarily reenlist, the Pentagon must rotate its forces in and out of theater every 12 months or so in order to maintain morale and reenlistment. Thus, just as a civilian police department must hire three to four police officers for every one cop on the beat, so too must the U.S. military have three to four soldiers for every one serving in Iraq.

The Pentagon, then, could have realistically kept those initial 250,000 to 300,000 troops in place only for a limited time—perhaps a year, certainly not more than two. That might have been enough time to pacify the country, especially if higher troop numbers at the outset would have quelled the early looting and disorder. Then again, a year or two might not have been sufficient time to beat back an insurgency which, we now know, was to some extent planned in advance of the invasion. In that case, keeping 250,000 to 300,000 troops in Iraq for two years or longer would have risked so lowering morale and reenlistment rates as to destroy the all-volunteer force. It would have been like plowing a field with a Ferrari; it could have been done, but only once.

Taking the need for rotations into account, then, the U.S. military can comfortably handle something like 80,000 troops in Iraq at any one time. The actual number on the ground has averaged 133,286 for the last two years, and more than 150,000 soldiers are in Iraq now.

That's a woefully insufficient number for the task. Yet it is pushing the outside limits of what the current force structure can handle. It has meant imposing "stop-loss" emergency measures to prevent soldiers from exiting the service. It has required deploying nearly every active-duty brigade, including one previously committed elsewhere in Korea. It has meant raiding the seed corn of military readiness by deploying the Army's elite "opposing force" training units—seasoned soldiers who play the enemy in mock exercises to build the skills of greener troops before they are sent into battle. It has necessitated calling up all 15 of the National Guard's enhanced readiness brigades, as well as poorly-resourced National Guard divisions that have not been mobilized *en masse* since the Korean War. It has led the Army Reserve Chief Lt. Gen. James Hemly to write in a recent memo that the Reserve will be unable to meet its commitments without substantial use of the Army's *involuntary* mobilization authorities under federal law. As of Dec. 15, 2004, the Army Reserve retained just 37,515 deployable soldiers out of a total of 200,366—almost no cushion at all. And in the final two months of last year, the Reserves missed their enlistment targets last year by 30 percent—a sign of even greater problems to come.

All this for a war that most planners consider to be a medium-sized conflict—nothing like what the United States faced in World War I, World War II, or the Cold War. And while threats of that magnitude aren't anywhere on the horizon, there are plenty of quite possible scenarios that could quickly overwhelm us—an implosion of the North Korean regime, a Chinese attack on Taiwan, worsening of the ethnic cleansing in the Sudan, or some unforeseen humanitarian nightmare. Already we have signaled to bad actors everywhere the limits of our power. Military threats might never have convinced the Iranians to give up their nuclear program. But it's more than a little troubling that ruling Iranian mullahs can publicly and credibly dismiss recent administration saber-rattling by pointing to the fact that our forces are pinned down in Iraq.

Stress Test

Every 20 years or so for the past century, America has found it necessary, for national security reasons, to send at least half a million troops overseas into harm's way, and to keep them there for years at a time. It did so in World War I, sending 4.1 million doughboys and Marines to Europe. In World War II, it mobilized 16 million for the war effort. America sent more than 3 million grunts to fight in Korea against the North Koreans and Chinese, in the first hot war of the Cold War. It rotated 5.1 million soldiers and Marines through Vietnam over a decade, with 543,400 stationed there at the height of that war in April 1969. And more recently, America sent 550,000 ground troops to eject Saddam's forces from Kuwait, as part of a ground force which totaled 831,500 with allied contributions from dozens of nations. Along the way; the United States military simultaneously fought small wars in Greece, Lebanon, El Salvador, Somalia, Haiti, Bosnia, and Kosovo, requiring the commitment of thousands more. This ability to deploy large numbers of troops overseas for long periods of time has been the price of America's superpower status—what President John Kennedy alluded to in his inaugural address when he said America would bear any burden to assure the survival and the success of liberty.

There's no reason to think that America will be exempt from paying that price in the future. Even those who don't support the Bush policy of using unilateral force to democratize the Middle East (and we don't), and who prefer to work through military alliances whenever possible (and we do), should understand the need to increase American troop strength. The international community failed to act in Rwanda largely because the United States chose not to send troops; our NATO allies sent soldiers into Bosnia and Kosovo only because we put substantial numbers of ours in, too. The same will hold true for just about any other major war or humanitarian intervention in the future.

What we're increasingly learning from Iraq is that the all-volunteer force, as presently built, cannot do that—indeed, it was consciously designed to be incapable of such deployments. Today's force was built for precisely the kinds of wars that Caspar Weinberger and Colin Powell envisioned in their doctrines: wars with explicit purposes, narrow parameters, and clear exit strategies. In other words, it was built for the kinds of wars the military prefers to fight, not necessarily the kinds of wars we have, as a nation, historically fought.

The evolution of this force owes much to Vietnam. After that war ended, the nation's senior generals devised a military structure called the "total force" concept to circumvent two of the great moral hazards they identified with Vietnam: the failure to mobilize the nation, with all of its strata and segments, for the war; and the reliance on young American conscripts, who were coerced by the state to kill or be killed.

Vietnam had been fought almost entirely by active-duty volunteers and conscripts. A great number of young men, including many from the nation's privileged classes, sought refuge in the reserves as

> *The modern American military came to embrace precision firepower over manpower in what historian Russell Weigley called the "American way of war."*

a way out of duty in Vietnam. The total force concept entailed, first of all, the splitting of key war-fighting and support functions. Henceforth, active-duty troops would perform nearly all the traditional combat roles; reservists would provide most of the support functions, such as logistics and military policing. This ensured that future wars could not be fought without the heavy involvement of the reserves. Army Gen. Creighton Abrams and other leaders felt that this would be a check on the power of presidents to go to war because mass reserve call-ups typically require a great deal of political capital.

Second, Pentagon leaders replaced the conscripted military with an all-volunteer force that would recruit enlistees with pay and benefits like the civilian world. This all-volunteer model, they believed, would improve morale for the simple reason that all soldiers would be in the service by choice. It would also improve military effectiveness because if soldiers could be lured to stay longer by reenlisting, they could acquire higher levels of skill. The mantra of the new military became "send a bullet, not a man"; the modern American military came to embrace precision firepower over manpower in what historian Russell Weigley called the "American way of war."

This all-volunteer military made good on nearly all these promises. After a rough period in the late 1970s, the U.S. military emerged a leaner, better force in the 1980s, proving itself in the small wars of that decade—Grenada, Libya, and Panama. Then came the first Gulf War—the apothesis of the all-volunteer, total force model. Coming off the Cold War, the Army had 18 divisions on active duty, in comparison to 10 today, and had little in the way of a pressing commission with the imminent collapse of the Soviet Union. By mobilizing seven of these Army divisions and two Marine divisions, in addition to the reserves and ready reserves, military leaders were able to send half a million troops to the Saudi desert. But because that war lasted just months, largely due to U.S. reluctance to invade and occupy Iraq, the system worked. Active-duty soldiers deployed for less than a year, without fear of immediately being sent back to fight; reservists were similarly tapped just once. Desert Storm did not break the all-volunteer force because that war was precisely the kind that the force had been designed to fight: a limited campaign for limited ends, of limited duration, and with a defined exit strategy.

Unfortunately, national security threats don't always conform to the military's precise specifications. The 1990s brought two wars, in Bosnia and Kosovo, requiring the long-term commitment of U.S. troops for peacekeeping. These were relatively modest-sized deployments. Yet the military leadership complained that they put undo stress on the system, and, indeed, then-Gov. George Bush lambasted the Clinton administration in 2000 for the way it managed military readiness, charging that the Kosovo war put two of the Army's 10 divisions out of action, hurting the nation's ability to respond to threats abroad. In the wake of September 11, the U.S. military mobilized tens of thousands of reservists for homeland security and sent thousands of elite infantrymen and special forces into the mountains of Afghanistan; neither mission conformed to the model of past wars.

Then came Operation Iraqi Freedom, and the real stress test began.

Five Bad Options

In theory, there are several ways to get out of the military manpower bind we find ourselves in. In reality, there are inherent limits to almost all of them.

The first option—at least the one Democrats and moderate Republicans have talked most about—is to convince other countries to share the burden in Iraq. But that's not likely. Even if the security situation in Iraq improves and the Bush administration begins to share decision-making—something it's so far refused to do—European leaders would be extremely wary of trying to sell their citizens on sending troops to keep the peace in a war they expressly opposed. It may be possible to convince the Europeans and other developed nations to be more willing to contribute troops the next time there's an international need. But that, as we've seen, will require more U.S. troops, not fewer. Nor should it be the policy of the United States to have to rely on other countries' troops. We must be prepared to intervene unilaterally if necessary.

A second solution to the manpower crisis would be to rely more on private military contractors, whose use has exploded in recent years. Currently, more than 40,000 government contractors are on duty in Iraq, working in myriad jobs from security to reconstruction. The advantage of using contractors is that they provide surge capacity; they are hired only for the duration of an engagement. But according to Peter W. Singer, a research fellow at the Brookings Institution, these private armies also create problems. First, all costs considered, they're not necessarily less expensive for the military. Second, private military contractors often compete with the military for personnel, so any growth in these contractors usually results in tension between military retention and contractor recruiting efforts. Third, contractors operate in a legal gray area where

> *The military cannot build additional capability simply by playing a shell game with its personnel; at some point, it must genuinely add more soldiers too, and in large numbers.*

their financial and accounting activities are heavily regulated, but their operations are barely looked at. It's one thing to contract for truck drivers; it's another to hire contractors to guard Afghan President Hamid Karzai or work as interrogation linguists in the Abu Ghraib prison because the military has too few commandos or linguists in its own ranks. The military has probably already pushed the contractor concept about as far as it will go; expecting much more surge capacity from private industry is probably unrealistic.

A third possibility might be to follow the advice of several cutting-edge military reformers to radically transform today's military. According to these reformers, today's force was drawn up for a bygone age of massed superpower armies; it does not reflect today's threats. These visionaries would downsize the Navy, scrap some of the Army's mechanized divisions, and in these and other ways free up tens of thousands of troops to be redeployed into "soldier centric" units capable of doing everything along the spectrum from humanitarian relief in Banda Aceh to combat patrols in Baghdad. Under pressure from the Iraq mission, the military has taken some steps in this direction—for instance, by retraining and reequipping some army artillery and air defense units into military police units. But such moves have been incremental in nature thus far; the true scope of the problem is orders of magnitude larger than the Pentagon's current solution. And some day, a war may come which requires all kinds of combat power—from large land-based formations to ships capable of sailing through the Taiwan strait to legions of peacekeepers. The military cannot build additional capability simply by playing a shell game with its personnel; at some point, it must genuinely add more soldiers too, and in large numbers.

A fourth option, and the most obvious one, would be to simply increase the size of the active-duty force. This too has been discussed. During the 2004 campaign, Sen. John Kerry called for increasing the active-duty force by 40,000 troops. More recently, a bipartisan group of hawkish defense intellectuals published an open letter on *The Weekly Standard* Web site calling on Congress to add 25,000 ground troops each year for the next several years. And the Pentagon has announced some money for extra troops in the administration's latest budget. The problem with such proposals is that they underestimate both current manpower needs and the cost of forcing the all-volunteer military to grow.

In theory, one can always lure the next recruit, or retain the next soldier, by offering a marginally higher monetary incentive—but in reality, there are practical limits to such measures. The pool of people who might be convinced to join the Army is mainly comprised of healthy young people with high school degrees but no college plans. That pool is inherently limited, especially when the economy is heating up and there's a shooting war on. Last year, despite signing bonuses in the tens of thousands and other perks, military recruiters had to lower entry standards to meet their enlistment goals. The active force met its recruiting targets for 2004, but the reserves have found themselves increasingly struggling to bring enough soldiers in the door.

But it's the long-term cost issues that most militate against making the all-volunteer force bigger. Generals today are fond of saying that you recruit a soldier, but you retain their families. One reason the Army has resisted Congress' attempts to raise its end strength is that it does not want to embrace all of the costs associated with permanently increasing the size of the military, because it sees each soldier as a 30-year commitment—both to the soldier and his (or her) family. According to the Congressional Budget Office, each soldier costs $99,000 per year—a figure which includes medical care, housing, and family benefits.

The United States does not necessarily need a massive standing military all the time. What it needs is a highly trained professional force of a certain size—what we have right now is fine—backed by a massive surge capacity of troops in reserve to quickly augment the active-duty force in times of emergency. Sure, right now, the Army is light several hundred thousand deployable ground troops. But over the long term, the demands of Iraq will subside, the need for troops will decline, and it could be another decade or two before another mission that big comes along.

The problem is that under the all-volunteer system it's hard to fix the short-term problem (too few troops now) without creating long-term problems (too many troops later). And so, paying for the salaries and benefits and families of 50,000 or 500,000 extra soldiers on active duty over the course of their careers doesn't, from a military standpoint, make sense. Politically, it would put the senior military leadership in the position of convincing the American people to keep military budgets extremely high to pay for a huge standing army that isn't being used and might not be for years. It might be possible now to convince the public to add another 100,000 soldiers (annual cost: about $10 billion in personnel costs alone, not including equipment and training). But the generals rightly worry that this support will evaporate after Iraq stabilizes. Indeed, Americans have a long tradition dating back to the writing of Constitution, of refusing to support a large standing military unless the need is apparent. (The public paid for a much bigger all-volunteer military in the 1970s and 1980s, but only because of the obvious need to deter a massive Soviet army from threatening Europe; after the Berlin Wall fell, both political parties supported big cuts in troop strength). What we really need is the capability to rapidly mobilize and deploy a half million troops to project U.S. power abroad, and to be able to sustain them indefinitely while maintaining a reserve with which to simultaneously engage other enemies.

Under the all-volunteer system it's hard to fix the short-term problem (too few troops now) without creating long-term problems (too many troops later).

A fifth option would be to build this surge capacity into the reserves, instead of the active force. Under this plan, which some military personnel planners are already discussing, the army would radically bump up enlistment bonuses and other incentives to lure vastly more young people directly into the reserves than are being recruited now. Such a plan would have the advantage of creating the surge capacity the nation needs without saddling the nation with a large, standing professional army. But the disadvantages are substantial, too. For such a plan to work, the military would have to make a commitment, which thus far it never has, to fix the legendary resources problems and anemic readiness of the reserves. A great many reservists have gone through the crucible of combat in Afghanistan and Iraq, and yet still cope with vehicles that lack armor, weapons older than they are, and a paucity of training dollars. Also, the army would always (and rightly) insist that signing bonuses for reservists be substantially below those offered to active-duty recruits. And even if bonuses and other renumeration for both the active-duty and the reserves were to rise substantially, it is hard to see how the reserves could lure in a sufficient number of recruits without significantly lowering admissions standards. The real advantage of the all-volunteer force is its quality. If the military tries to recruit so many soldiers that it must substantially lower its entry requirements, then the all-volunteer force will lose its qualitative edge. This decrease in quality will have a cascade effect on discipline within the ranks, degrading combat effectiveness for these units.

A 21st-century Draft

That leaves one option left for providing the military with sufficient numbers of high-quality deployable ground forces: conscription. America has nearly always chosen this option to staff its military in times of war. Today, no leading politician in either party will come anywhere near the idea—the draft having replaced Social Security as the third rail of American politics. This will have to change if the United States is to remain the world's preeminent power.

Traditional conscription has its obvious downsides. On a practical level, draftees tend to be less motivated than volunteers. Because they serve for relatively short periods of time (typically two years), any investment made in their training is lost to the military once the draftees return to civilian life. And despite the current manpower shortage, there's no foreseeable scenario in which all 28 million young Americans currently of draft age would be needed.

Above all else, there's the serious ethical problem that conscription means government compelling young adults to risk death, and to kill—an act of the state that seems contrary to the basic notions of liberty which animate our society.

The real advantage of the all-volunteer force is its quality.

In practice, however, our republic has decided many times throughout its history that a draft was necessary to protect those basic liberties. Even if you disagreed with the decision to invasion of Iraq, or think the president's rhetoric is demagogic and his policies disastrous, it is hard to argue that Islamic terrorism isn't a threat to freedom and security, at home and abroad. Moreover, any American, liberal or conservative, ought to have moral qualms about basing our nation's security on an all-volunteer force drawn disproportionately, as ours is, from America's lower socioeconomic classes. And the cost of today's war is being borne by an extremely narrow slice of America. Camp Pendleton, Calif., home to the 1st Marine Expeditionary Force, is also home to approximately one-seventh of the U.S. fatalities from Iraq. In theory, our democracy will not fight unpopular wars because the people who must bear the casualties can impose their will on our elected leaders to end a war they do not support. But when such a small fraction of America shoulders the burden—and pays the cost—of America's wars, this democratic system breaks down.

Nor are the practical considerations of a draft impossible to overcome. A draft lottery, of the kind that existed in the peacetime draft of the 1950s, with no exemptions for college students, would provide the military an appropriate and manageable amount of manpower without the class inequities that poisoned the national culture during Vietnam. Such a system, however, would not avoid the problem of flooding the military with less-than-fully-motivated conscripts.

A better solution would fix the weaknesses of the all-volunteer force without undermining its strengths. Here's how such a plan might work. Instead of a lottery, the federal government would impose a requirement that no four-year college or university be allowed to accept a student, male or female, unless and until that student had completed a 12-month to two-year term of service. Unlike an old-fashioned draft, this 21st-century service requirement would provide a vital element of personal choice. Students could choose to fulfill their obligations in any of three ways: in national service programs like AmeriCorps (tutoring disadvantaged children), in homeland security assignments (guarding ports), or in the military. Those who chose the latter could serve as military police officers, truck drivers, or other non-combat specialists requiring only modest levels of training. (It should be noted that the Army currently offers two-year enlistments for all of these jobs, as well as for the infantry.) They would be deployed as needed for peacekeeping or nation-building missions. They would serve for 12-months to two years, with modest follow-on reserve obligations.

Whichever option they choose, all who serve would receive modest stipends and GI Bill–type college grants. Those who sign up for lengthier and riskier duty, however, would receive higher pay and larger college grants. Most would no doubt pick the less dangerous options. But some would certainly select the military—out of patriotism, a sense of adventure, or to test their mettle. Even if only 10 percent of the one-million young people who annually start at four-year colleges and universities were to choose the military option, the armed forces would receive 100,000 fresh recruits every year. These would be motivated recruits, having chosen the military over other, less demanding forms of service. And because they would all be college-grade and college-bound, they would have—to a greater extent than your average volunteer recruit—the savvy and inclination to pick up foreign languages and other skills that are often the key to effective peacekeeping work.

A 21st-century draft like this would create a cascading series of benefits for society. It would instill a new ethic of service in that sector of society, the college-bound, most likely to reap the fruits of American prosperity. It would mobilize an army of young people for vital domestic missions, such as helping a growing population of seniors who want to avoid nursing homes but need help with simple daily tasks like grocery shopping. It would give more of America's elite an experience of the military. Above all, it would provide the all-important surge capacity now missing from our force structure, insuring that the military would never again lack for manpower. And it would do all this without requiring any American to carry a gun who did not choose to do so.

The war in Iraq has shown us, and the world, many things: the bloody costs of inept leadership; the courage of the average American soldier; the hunger for democracy among some of the earth's most oppressed people. But perhaps more than anything, Iraq has shown that our military power has limits. As currently constituted, the U.S. military can win the wars, but it cannot win the peace, nor can it commit for the long term to the stability and security of a nation such as Iraq. Our enemies have learned this, and they will use that knowledge to their advantage in the next war to tie us down and bleed us until we lose the political will to fight.

If America wishes to retain its mantle of global leadership, it must develop a military force structure capable of persevering under these circumstances. Fortunately, we know how to build such a force. We have done it many times in the past. The question is: Do we have the will to do so again?

An Army of the Willing

By Richard A. Posner
The New Republic, May 19, 2003

In the theory of the state that John Stuart Mill sketched in *On Liberty*, the government's role is to provide an unobtrusive framework for private activities. Government provides certain goods, such as national defense and (in some versions) education, that private markets will not provide in sufficient quantities. But beyond that it merely protects a handful of entitlements (property rights and some personal liberties) that are necessary to prevent markets from not working at all or from running off the rails, as would happen, for example, if there were no sanctions for theft. Limited government so conceived—the conception most commonly called "nineteenth-century liberalism," to distinguish it from modern welfare liberalism—has no ideology, no "projects," but is really just an association for mutual protection.

Since the election of Ronald Reagan in 1980, and with scarcely a beat skipped during the presidency of Bill Clinton, the United States—by such means as widespread privatization and deregulation, welfare reform, and indifference to growing inequalities of income—has been experimenting with a partial return to nineteenth-century liberalism. This development is obscured by the fact that the left believes in personal but not economic liberty, and that the right believes in economic but not personal liberty, and that the Millian center, which believes in both forms of liberty, has no articulate presence in either of the major political parties. But since the left has been notably unsuccessful in restricting economic liberty, and the right has been largely unsuccessful in restricting personal liberty, what we have in fact, though it is rarely acknowledged, is an approximation, though a very rough one, to a Millian polity.

The most sweeping intellectual challenge to our reviving nineteenth-century liberalism comes not from the dwindling band of socialists, with their narrow focus on economic issues, or from the social or religious conservatives, with their narrow focus on abortion, homosexuality, religion, and a handful of other purely "social" issues, but from the communitarians. These political theorists think that liberalism as practiced in the United States today is causing people to lose all sense of communal responsibility. They argue that people are becoming self-preoccupied and thus indifferent to the claims of the community. As evidence they point to our high rates of crime and divorce and out-of-wedlock births; and to our declining rates of participation in communal activities such as voting; and even to the prevalence of commuting and the popularity of television-watching because these (the first especially) tend to be solitary activities.

For many communitarians, the demon is commodification—the substitution of market services for non-market services. Private prisons, private tutors for four-year-olds applying for admission to $17,000-per-year New York City kindergartens, Duke University's sale of freshman places to rich kids, professional dog walkers, the auction of the electromagnetic spectrum, and surrogate-motherhood contracts: these are some of the gaudier examples. Of greater significance is paid child care, though those communitarians who are liberals in the modern sense do not care to dwell on this point. No longer do mothers feel morally obligated to take full-time care of their children themselves, or grandparents to step in for a busy or absent parent. The purchase of child care is now a legitimate option. The care of the elderly has to a great extent been shucked off to retirement and nursing homes supported by Social Security. And no longer is military service an obligation of citizenship. There is no draft; the army is a career like any other. Preoccupied with money-making and other private projects, many people evade taxes and jury duty, and in most elections fewer than half the eligible voters bother to vote.

To the practical-minded, the communitarian movement founders on a dearth of useful suggestions for reversing—or even just slowing—the dismal decline that the communitarians bemoan. Most of their proposals echo those made by others on grounds unrelated to communitarianism. One does not have to be a communitarian to want safe, clean parks or high standards in education. Their distinctive proposals tend toward the quixotic, as in Robert Putnam's proposal for an annual Jane Addams Award for "the Gen X'er or Gen Y'er who comes up with the best idea" for restoring social capital; or to the unlovely, as in Michael Lind's program of "liberal nationalism," which proposes restricting immigration and using tariffs to prevent foreign countries from competing with us on the basis of lower wage rates in those countries. But the dominant communitarian note is banality, as when Putnam in *Bowling Alone* says (in italics—so important did he consider the point), "Let us find ways to ensure that by 2010 Americans will spend less leisure time sitting passively alone in front of a glowing screen and more time in active connection with our fellow citizens."

But there is a deeper problem with communitarian thinking than the lack of a constructive agenda. Its diagnosis of the nation's ills is empirically off. We know this because in recent years, at the same time that the ties of community as they are imagined by communitarians have been fraying, the ills to which that fraying was thought to give rise have been abating rather than increasing. Crime rates have fallen, as have rates of abortion, teenage births, and births out of wedlock; welfare dependency has declined; racial tension is significantly reduced. The causality is complex; but the communitarians owe us an explanation for why their predictions have been falsified. A possible answer that they will not like is that commodification promotes prosperity and prosperity alleviates social ills. Think of the social and economic implications of abolishing life insurance, which commodifies human life; or re-instituting the draft or imposing other compulsory national service, which would deprive the economy of a significant slice of its productive labor; or ending Social Security and child care subsidies in order to strengthen the family. Not that many communitarians would endorse all these measures, but nothing in their theory tells them when to stop turning back the clock.

In a lecture in 1998 titled "What Money Can't Buy," Michael Sandel observed that "to turn [military] service into a commodity—a job for pay—is to corrupt or degrade the sense of civic virtue that properly attends it." To Sandel—here following Rousseau, who had said, "I hold enforced labor to be less opposed to liberty than taxes"—the volunteer army is a prime example of rampant and destructive commodification. The suggestion is perverse. Conscription could be described as a form of slavery, in the sense that a conscript is a person deprived of the ownership of his own labor; and slavery is the ultimate commodification, because it treats a human being as a salable good. Michael Lind likewise had it backward when he opposed the volunteer army (which he had called a "mercenary" force) on the ground that "in a republic, as opposed to the old-fashioned despotic monarchies, the citizens participate, they are the owners of the state, the state does not own them." But surely it is conscription that treats the persons conscripted as if the state does own them. There are circumstances in which military service is an obligation of citizenship, but ownership is a poor metaphor for obligation. The state that asserts an unlimited right to the enforced labor of its people is not participatory, it is despotic.

The volunteer army was not the brainchild of Milton Friedman and other commodifiers. We have had a volunteer army for most of our history, conscription having long been resisted here, as in England, as a Continental practice associated with Napoleonic militarism. The volunteer army was re-instituted when there was no longer a felt need for a mass of (inevitably sullen) cannon fodder. The criticisms of it by the communitarians are refuted by the public response to it in the recent war with Iraq. Only the Iraqi minister of information described our soldiers as "mercenaries." No American was heard to say that since our soldiers are paid to risk their lives, we should regard the death, the wounding, or the capture of them with the same equanimity with which we regard the occasional death and maiming of race-car drivers, lion tamers, and mountain climbers. No American was heard to say, and I doubt that any American thought, that one reason to regret heavy American casualties was that it might force up the wages necessary to attract people to a military career. The armed forces are regarded with unstinted admiration, and the recovery of the handful of captured American soldiers was greeted with national rejoicing. To contend that the voluntary character of the American military degrades the concept of American citizenship would strike most Americans as daft.

It is true, as Sandel has emphasized, that the enlisted men and women in the armed forces (as distinct from the officers) are drawn primarily from the lower middle class and so are not a perfect cross-section of the American population. He regards them as "coerced" by economic necessity to volunteer, just as if they were drafted. This is far-fetched, and a similar sentiment was expressed by Representative Charles Rangel of New York in April when he remarked, "If our great nation becomes involved in an all-out war, the sacrifice must be equally shared. It is apparent that service in the armed services of our nation is not a common experience for our youth and that disproportionate numbers of the poor and members of minority groups compose the enlisted ranks of the military while the sons and daughters of the most privileged Americans are underrepresented or absent. We must return to the tradition of the citizen-soldier." This, too, is far-fetched. The true consequence of the demographics of the armed forces—a consequence that communitarians should applaud—is that the nation's admiration for these scions of the lower middle class helps to bind the different income classes together. The military prowess of the United States is recognized to be the joint product of the technological and organizational prowess of wealthy corporations, high-paid executives, and highly educated scientists and engineers, on the one hand, and the courage, competence, and high spirits of the young people from the other side of the tracks (to make the point rather too dramatically) who dominate the enlisted ranks. I suspect, by the way, that many television-watchers found the privates, non-commissioned officers, and junior officers more impressive than the generals; and this was an egalitarian lesson delivered by commodification. "The general critique of the 1990s was that we had raised a generation with peroxide hair and tongue rings, general illiterates who lounged at malls, occasionally muttering 'like' and 'you know' in Sean Penn or Valley Girl cadences," Victor Hanson Davis has remarked. "But somehow the military has married the familiarity and dynamism of crass popular culture to nineteenth-century notions of heroism, self-sacrifice, patriotism, and audacity."

A notable omission in the communitarian criticism of the volunteer army is the failure to consider that a professional army (a term synonymous with volunteer army) is likely to be much more

> *To contend that the voluntary character of the American military degrades the concept of American citizenship would strike most Americans as daft.*

effective militarily than a conscript army under current conditions of warfare. How much military effectiveness should we give up to promote the communitarian vision? The communitarians have not told us. There is a subtler significance of the shift from a conscript to a professional army that they also ignore. As David King and Zachary Karabell pointed out in *The Generation of Trust*, one reason for the enhanced esteem in which our volunteer military is held compared to its conscript predecessor is that when labor is hired rather than conscripted, the employer must persuade the labor pool that working for him is attractive. When it could no longer rely on the draft to fill its ranks, the military conducted large-scale advertising and marketing campaigns to attract recruits and had great success with its slogan "Be All That You Can Be." Most of the people who saw the ads were not potential recruits, but they, too, were impressed, and so the ads helped to change the negative image that the public had of the military as a result of the Vietnam fiasco.

So here was another dividend of commodification, and not an adventitious one either. For one of the differences between allocating resources, human and otherwise, by means of the market (which is all that communitarians mean by "commodification") and using coercion to allocate them is that the former method fosters cooperation. Indeed, it fosters a form of community. Unable any longer to obtain labor by force, the military was compelled to transform itself into an institution that people would respect and trust. Bonds forged by trust replaced bonds forged by fear of punishment. It is what one might have thought communitarians would have wanted.

Schroder to End Conscription in Push for EU Rapid Reaction Force

By Tony Paterson
The Sunday Telegraph (London), April 13, 2003

Germany is poised to abolish military conscription and reduce its army by a third in a move that it hopes will strengthen Europe's defences and reduce dependence on America after the Iraq war.

The government of Chancellor Gerhard Schroder is drawing up plans to cut troops over the next five years from about 300,000 to 200,000, leading to a fully professional armed force like that in Britain.

The plan is part of a Franco-German drive to boost the European defence force, which took over peacekeeping duties from Nato last week in the former Yugoslav republic of Macedonia.

Winfried Nachtwei, an MP in Mr. Schroder's coalition who specialises in defence matters, said that the plan would be finalised "by the end of the year." He added: "Mr. Schroder is convinced that conscription is an anachronism which has no place in a modern German army if it is to face today's challenges."

Although ending conscription would add to Germany's high unemployment rate, Mr. Schroder calculates that it would be popular with 100,000 18-year-old men compelled to join the armed forces each year. An equal number of young men opt for community service as an alternative.

His plan is a key element in a Franco-German initiative to bolster the 60,000-strong European rapid reaction force, agreed with Britain's backing at the EU's 1999 Helsinki summit but which so far has failed to materialise in any significant form.

The rift over Iraq—which has divided "old Europe" from America and Britain—has prompted France and Germany to redouble their efforts to set up a European force to act as a counterweight to America's global military dominance.

President Chirac and Chancellor Schroder are holding a special summit in Brussels this month with leaders of Belgium and Luxembourg to hasten its implementation. All four countries opposed the Iraq war but insist that the new force will strengthen rather than weaken Nato. Last week Chancellor Schroder, one of the most

---

Article by Tony Paterson from *The Sunday Telegraph*, April 13, 2003. Copyright © *The Sunday Telegraph*. Reprinted with permission.

vociferous European critics of American policy in Iraq, said: "Given the imbalances in the world it would be fatal if Europe did not live up to its responsibilities."

The abolition of conscription will be a historic milestone. Since the Second World War German politicians have been wedded to the idea that conscription would prevent the armed forces from ever being subverted by a totalitarian regime. However, since the collapse of communism, the German military—the largest in Europe—has proved ill-equipped, underfunded and oversized.

German forces have been effective in peacekeeping operations in the Balkans and Afghanistan but serious doubts have been raised about their structure. Two years ago a government commission concluded: "In their present form the German armed forces have no future. They are too big, improperly structured and increasingly old-fashioned." Yet until now there has been little military reform.

Berlin spends 26.9 billion euros (pounds 18.5 billion) annually to fund an army of 308,000 men, compared to the pounds 24 billion spent by Britain on its 211,000-strong Armed Forces. Germany is also one of the last countries in Europe to practise conscription, with recruits each having to serve for nine months. Last week the German government announced that it may reduce the term to six months in a first step towards abolition.

The end of conscription would release an estimated 1 billion euros each year, which could be spent on modernising the armed forces. More than half of the German defence budget is devoted to salaries and benefits for the armed forces' 130,000 civilian personnel. Under German law, any civilian who has worked for the army for more than 15 years is almost impossible to dismiss, and Mr. Schroder's government abandoned an attempt to cut civilian numbers last year after meeting stiff union opposition.

The German armed forces also suffer from a shortage of military hardware, which limits its potential contribution to the new Euro-army. Its forces have few precision-guided weapons and an outdated battlefield command and control system—and lack the means to transport troops far beyond its borders.

Failure of Chancellor Schroder's government to invest in modernising the armed forces has prompted criticism from senior army officers. One former German army general, Klaus Naumann, who until recently was chairman of Nato's military committee, said: "We need to spend much more on capital investment. Six to eight per cent of the budget needs to be freed up now, otherwise the modernisation won't happen fast enough."

III. Youth and the Draft

Editor's Introduction

In contrast with the previous chapter, the pieces in this section focus on the thoughts and concerns of the young people who would be called upon to serve should conscription be reestablished. The articles include interviews with teens as well as polls charting the opinions of young people. This data suggests that both proponents and detractors of national service recognize that young people seem to be almost unanimously against mandatory conscription.

In "Considering the Draft," Max Friedman, a high-school student, specifically addresses Congressman Rangel's conscription legislation. Friedman writes, "The most effective way to increase the army's effectiveness is clear, and it is not the draft. If the pay and benefits of being a soldier were better, more people would be interested in joining the military." He also points out that conscription could undermine Rangel's goal of achieving a military more representative of the American populace. "The rich and privileged of America will find ways to avoid the draft," Friedman contends, "but the less affluent will have no choice but to serve if their number comes up. A system of selective service where not everyone has to serve is divisive."

"Well, No, They Won't Go," by John Cook, profiles Charlie Moskos, a sociology professor at Northwestern University, who, next to Rangel, is perhaps the most well-known proponent of reinstating the draft. Cook describes Moskos as one of the most popular professors on campus. When his students are asked to comment on his opinions on conscription, however, they are quick to disagree with him. The piece contrasts the views of the students—one of whom says she feels "exempt" from service, while another insists that a draft would "disrupt my life"—with Moskos's assertion that "those who benefit most from society should be the ones with their lives on the line. I would start the draft at the top of the social ladder." Cook writes that Moskos is "surprisingly sanguine about his students' attitudes. He doesn't blame them so much as the culture of self-regard in which they have been raised."

In "Young People Fear Return of Military Draft," Marian Gail Brown describes individual students at a Connecticut high school and their anxieties about military service. Brown evokes a student body that is generally well informed about the politics of the war and critical of the U.S. presence in Iraq. Brown quotes one student who says, "There's far too much confusion over there. Do we know what we are fighting for there [in Iraq] to risk more people losing their lives? . . . I have lots of respect for the troops that are there. But I think about the idea of a draft all the time now. And the last thing I would want to do is go to war for something I didn't believe in."

Finally, Dennis Welch, in "Teens Frown on National Service Requirement," discusses a Gallup poll in which 57 percent of young people between the ages of 13 and 17 oppose a requirement for "all men and women to give one year of service to the nation, either in military or non-military work, such as work in hospitals or with elderly people." The poll also reveals that young Republicans are slightly more likely than young Democrats to favor a national service requirement.

Considering the Draft

BY MAX FRIEDMAN
WINSTON-SALEM JOURNAL, JULY 5, 2004

"No state has an inherent right to survive through conscript troops and, in the long run, no state ever has," wrote Henry Adams, a historian, journalist and novelist who lived through the Civil War.

The draft bill currently before Congress, known as the "Universal National Service Act of 2003," has reopened the issue of selective service nearly 30 years after it was terminated.

Needless to say, few have lent support to the bill, because, based on information from past uses of selective service, drafts tend to weaken society and the military.

For these same reasons, I also believe the draft is the wrong course of action for our country to take to strengthen our military.

History tells us that military drafts divide the nation and create enmities, just as they have during most drafts since the Civil War. According to Christopher Jehn, a former director of the Marine Corps Operations Analysis Group at the Center for Naval Analyses in Alexandria, Va., the draft actually weakens society. In an essay found on the Concise Encyclopedia of Economics Web site (www.econlib.org), Jehn writes that the draft causes "wasteful avoidance behavior like the unwanted schooling, emigration, early marriages and distorted career choices of the 50s and 60s."

In addition, the rich and privileged of America will find ways to avoid the draft, but the less affluent will have no choice but to serve if their number comes up. A system of selective service where not everyone has to serve is divisive.

The damage to the nation, however, does not end at its division between the privileged and the poor. The military suffers as well.

The draft, by nature, forces men and women into situations they did not choose. U.S. Rep. Ron Paul, R-Texas, said in a speech to Congress in 2002 that feuds develop between those forced into the armed forces and those who volunteer. He said that this "undermines the cohesiveness of military units, which is a vital element of military effectiveness." Because the soldiers in an army of conscripts are not in place by choice, the army as a whole ends up with low morale.

Article by Max Friedman from the *Winston-Salem Journal*, July 5, 2004. Copyright © *Winston-Salem Journal*. Reprinted with permission.

There are hundreds of thousands of men in active service, the National Guard and the reserves. All are volunteers. Each and every man and woman in the service chose to don the uniform, agreed to fight for America and decided to take orders. A person forced into the army is not there by choice, and, therefore, may resent his or her position. Someone who knows that he or she is there for only a short time is more likely to work just to survive until the conscription is complete.

This sort of changeover in the motivational drive of soldiers was evident toward the end of Vietnam when soldiers began to realize that the objective was no longer to push forward but to pull out. The same sort of motivational weakness will undoubtedly develop in troops drafted in the future.

Jehn also points out that, since the military has adopted an all-volunteer force, the quality of our troops has risen significantly. Not only are our troops, on average, more educated, but there are also fewer discipline problems, greater retention (resulting in greater experience) and a much greater overall strength in versatility and ability.

A draft would result in a loss of these excellent statistics, and, more important, because of the reduced experience that troops would have, casualties on the battlefield would rise. The best determinant of survival on the battlefield is experience, just as experience is the best determinant of success in any job. Inexperienced troops and a dangerous battleground do not mix.

The most effective way to increase the army's effectiveness is clear, and it is not the draft. If the pay and benefits of being a soldier were better, more people would be interested in joining the military.

Another important fact that remains is that a draft does not save money, despite the fact that, historically, the military pays draftees less than other recruits. Training costs alone would outweigh any savings made on draftee pay cuts.

Needless to say, the country does not need a draft that causes so many problems for everyone involved. In addition, it is historically evident that the consequences of a draft would have such far-reaching consequences that America would be stuck with both a weakened military and damaged society for years to come.

Well, No, They Won't Go

BY JOHN COOK
CHICAGO TRIBUNE, DECEMBER 1, 2002

On a flawless autumn afternoon on the campus of Northwestern University, Charlie Moskos was preparing for battle. He surveyed the 600 or so students arrayed before him outside Leverone Auditorium and launched into a rallying cry. "We can take them!" he said. "There's more of us!"

Inside the hall, an unsuspecting professor was lecturing on what sounded like the history of ancient Greece. He and his class were on the wrong end of a scheduling mix-up; Moskos had reserved the room for his class. And now came Charlie Moskos charging through the door with 600 underclassmen at his back.

Carnage was avoided at the last possible moment when the Greek scholars agreed to vacate in 10 minutes.

At 68, Moskos, a self-described "short, fat, and bald" Northwestern sociology professor, is not quite the picture of the dashing field marshal. But he is an Army veteran, former war correspondent and longtime student of the military. And once he and the students in his Sociology 110 class have occupied the auditorium, he will try to argue to 600 overachieving future professionals why they all ought to be drafted after they graduate.

Northwestern students love Charlie Moskos—his introduction to sociology is one of the university's most popular courses. But a draft?

"It would disrupt my life," said one freshman before class, making clear by her tone that she would rather her life not be disrupted.

"I can die for my country," said another, incredulously, "but I can't drink a beer in my own house?"

Perhaps not surprisingly, much of America's younger generation would rather drink beer in their own houses than die for their country.

In the immediate aftermath of the Sept. 11 attacks, many observers quite reasonably assumed that the ensuing surge in patriotic sentiments would galvanize young men and women to enlist in the armed forces in record numbers. Not so. Flags went up in car windows, but eligible patriots did not show up in significant numbers at recruitment centers.

Copyrighted 12/1/2002, Chicago Tribune Company. All rights reserved. Used with permission.

According to a survey of Northwestern and University of Illinois at Chicago students that Moskos conducted for the Army, on the whole, Sept. 11 made college students slightly less willing to sign up than they had been before the attacks.

As the country lurches day by day toward war in Iraq, the Department of Defense maintains that its current troop levels are adequate to the tasks at hand, though the service branches increasingly are calling on reserves to meet manpower needs, and will almost certainly need to call up tens of thousands of reserve troops should an invasion of Iraq become necessary.

But at the same time, the military is taking great pains to find new ways to market itself to potential recruits—from the $147 million per year "Army of One" ad campaign, launched in January of last year by the Chicago-based advertising firm Leo Burnett, to "America's Army," a video game commissioned and distributed for free by the Army and designed to offer civilians "an inside perspective and a virtual role in today's premiere land force."

> *[Charlie] Moskos is the first to admit that his ideas on resurrecting the draft are highly unlikely to become reality anytime soon.*

Then there's "Enduring Freedom," a documentary short commissioned by the Navy and the Marines that includes footage of U.S. troops engaged in battle in Afghanistan and was shown as a trailer to moviegoers across the nation.

And let's not forget the Marines' decision to sponsor NASCAR drivers.

Moskos has an answer, of course. Don't recruit young people. Draft them. Moskos was himself drafted in 1956, shortly after he graduated from Princeton University, and he recalls the experience with nostalgia.

He was exposed to people and places that a cloistered Ivy Leaguer would usually never see. The experience led him to devote his life to studying public service—both military and civilian, such as the Peace Corps—and how to convince America's youth that it is worthwhile.

Moskos is the first to admit that his ideas on resurrecting the draft are highly unlikely to become reality anytime soon, but he is no egghead academic laboring in a sociological fantasyland—his ideas about civilian service led in part to the creation of Bill Clinton's AmeriCorps.

He wants to draft college graduates and give them three options: military service, a civilian service program along the lines of AmeriCorps or enlistment in the newly created Department of Homeland Security.

Back in the lecture hall, after mulling aloud over the staffing obstacles facing the new department, which will employ roughly 160,000 people, Moskos put it to his students this way: "To me, the answer to homeland security should be"—he raised a hand from the lectern, index finger extended toward the students—"you!"

But the students have someone else—anyone else—in mind. They are, admittedly, a highly unrepresentative sample of the nation's youth—being Northwestern students, they are unusually bright and drawn largely from comfortable backgrounds—but the students who stuck around after Moskos' pitch to talk to a reporter were remarkably blunt about their aversion to military or any other type of public service.

"I feel like we're exempt, in a weird way," said Ashley Mason, a freshman from Chicago.

The consensus seemed to be that military service is coarse, down-market and better suited to people who have neither the intellectual nor the financial means to attend a first-rate school.

"It's not like it's going to bring honor to your family," said Dannah Schinder, a freshman from Minneapolis. "Upper-class people think they're better than that."

"My parents would be freaked out if I joined the Army," said Josh Wagner, a freshman from White Plains, N.Y. "They're pretty set on me going to college."

Of course you can do both. Christiane Grant of Naperville, a third-year cadet at the U.S. Coast Guard Academy, is getting an engineering education in exchange for promising to spend five years patrolling our shores in the Coast Guard.

"I was actually tired of school," said Grant via e-mail (cadets don't have ready access to telephones), explaining her decision to attend a service academy.

"I wanted to do something that was new and exciting. Going to a civilian college seemed like a four-year rerun of high school just to punch the ticket and get a college degree."

Grant hopes to go on to a career in the Coast Guard, but she acknowledges that the military isn't for everyone, and doesn't support a draft.

"I have never felt an obligation to serve my country," she says. "'Obligation' sounds so negative. I have, however, always felt a strong desire to be useful to my country. Serving in the military is not the only way to serve your country."

Perhaps it shouldn't come as a surprise that there is a certain mistrust of military culture on a college campus such as Northwestern, but a similar attitude prevails when the topic turns to the civil-service component of Moskos' plan.

"My cousin was in the Peace Corps, and she loved it," said Danielle Carlson, a freshman from Oak Forest. "But when I hear stories about maggots in her food—I don't know. If it comes down to dying of bacteria in a foreign country, or dying of a bullet in a foreign country, you have to be really dedicated to risk your life like that. And I wouldn't be very good at that."

For a booster of military and civilian service, Moskos is surprisingly sanguine about his students' attitudes. He doesn't blame them so much as the culture of self-regard in which they have been raised.

"Nobody has asked them to serve—that's the point," he said. "It's virtual honor—'yeah, it's good to be in the military, but not me.' Well, those who benefit most from society should be the ones with their lives on the line. I would start the draft at the top of the social ladder."

Short of a draft, Moskos said, the key to inspiring voluntary service is the right role models. He likes to repeat an anecdote about a conference of military recruiters he attended in the early 1990s. He asked the assembled recruiters which they would prefer: a three-fold increase in their marketing budgets or for Chelsea Clinton to enlist. Almost all voted for the latter.

In Moskos' day, Elvis Presley's stint in the Army—as a draftee—was a boon to recruiters. Today, Moskos has another pop idol in mind.

"Just think," he said wistfully, "if Eminem joined the Army today. Just think what that would mean."

Young People Fear Return of Military Draft

By Marian Gail Brown
Connecticut Post, June 14, 2004

Giancarlo Marotti not only sensed fear inside Fairfield Warde High School teacher Amy Handy's advanced placement English class, he saw it and he touched it, too. So did the rest of his classmates.

The assignment this particular day was for students to bring in an object that for them symbolized fear. Marotti arrived at the first-period class with a newspaper photograph of an American soldier in Iraq.

"It was at a lookout camp. He looked tense, tired, too, maybe," Marotti says. "It scared me because I looked at this picture and I think 'this could be me. This could be me in less than two years because I will be 18 and out of high school.'"

Around Marotti, many other juniors in Handy's classroom are aware that two bills in Congress aim to reinstate the military draft could conscribe them to a two-year tour of duty. And unlike the draft during the Vietnam era, as one of the bills is presently worded, the Universal National Service Act would contain no exemption for college students.

All men and women between the ages of 18 and 26 would have to serve in some form of national service, not necessarily a combat position, for a minimum of two years.

"My parents don't support what's going on [in Iraq.] And they'd feel I was putting my life in danger if I went," Marotti says. "So, I would have to seriously contemplate heading to Canada or Italy or someplace. My parents wouldn't want me to go to war. So I know that they'd support what I had to do."

Marotti's friend and classmate Clara Davis, 17, nods in agreement. She reads the newspaper, listens to what politicians have to say about the war on terror and talks to her friends. Passage of a military draft for the first time since Vietnam is "unnecessary" because there are enough troops there now, she says.

"There's far too much confusion over there. Do we know what we are fighting for there [in Iraq] to risk more people losing their lives?" Davis says. "I have lots of respect for the troops that are

© 2004 *Connecticut Post* (Used with permission)

there. But I think about the idea of a draft all the time now. And the last thing I would want to do is go to war for something I didn't believe in. I should be able to go to college, not Iraq."

Jesse Habansky, a 26-year-old writer from Bridgeport, marvels at the level of knowledge, sophistication and political discourse among not just college students, but high school ones as well.

"They're more educated about what's happening than in the Vietnam War days," Habansky says. "They listen to alternative radio and N[ational] P[ublic] R[adio], they know what's going on. I see so many kids say 'I know what's going on over there. There's no need to send any more troops. We have enough there.'"

Forty percent of the nation's Army reservists and National Guard units are stationed in Iraq. And many of them have been notified that their tour of duty is being extended because of ongoing terrorism threats and insurgencies.

While the idea of an all-volunteer military may be popular with the Pentagon, it hasn't proven strong enough to draw enough recruits for the war in Iraq. So, the Reserves have had to make up the difference, by increasingly shouldering the active-duty burden.

Interestingly, the one issue that both supporters and opponents of the war on terror agree on appears to be the issue of conscription. They all oppose it.

J. P. Rizzitelli, a 28-year-old former Army combat engineer from Derby, believes that right now the supply of troops outpaces demand.

"The chance of a draft being reinstated would be small, infinitely small," Rizzitelli says. "If it came to the draft gaining passage, I don't think it would be received well. Anytime the government forces anything, it doesn't go over well."

Nevertheless, Rizzitelli says, "if it was necessary, I'd be all for it. What it takes to win a war is atrocious. But if we don't, the outcome will be so much worse."

Teens Frown on National Service Requirement

By Dennis Welch
Gallup Poll Tuesday Briefing, May 11, 2004

Last year, the Universal National Service Act of 2003 was introduced in both the U.S. House and Senate. If passed, the act would require every American citizen between the ages of 18 and 26 to provide two years of service to the nation. In the language of the bill itself, participants would perform their service either 1) "as a member of an active or reserve component of the uniformed services," or 2) "in a civilian capacity that, as determined by the President, promotes the national defense, including national or community service and homeland security."

Although the bill has not progressed out of committee, how would American teenagers feel about performing required national service? A new Gallup Youth Survey* asked teens if they would favor or oppose requiring "all men and women to give one year of service to the nation, either in military or non-military work, such as work in hospitals or with elderly people." More than half (57%) of teens (aged 13 to 17) said they would oppose such a requirement, while a substantial minority, 42%, would favor it.

Influence of War

Although both the text of the National Service Act and the Gallup question encompass both military and non-military service, the current war in Iraq might dissuade teens from favoring a national service requirement. Understandably, any mention of required military service might instill fear in the minds of young people. The debate continues about whether the current U.S. military is large enough, and there is even some talk about reinstituting the draft. In a recent speech, Republican Sen. Chuck Hagel of Nebraska said that the country should "begin exploring its options" regarding mandatory military service.

Copyright © 2004 The Gallup Organization. All rights reserved. Reprinted with permission.

* The Gallup Youth Survey is conducted via an Internet methodology provided by Knowledge Networks, using an online research panel that is designed to be representative of the entire U.S. population. The current questionnaire was completed by 785 respondents, aged 13 to 17, between Jan. 22 and March 9, 2004. For results based on the total sample, one can say with 95% confidence that the maximum margin of sampling error is +/-4 percentage points.

The poll shows that teens are apparently unenthusiastic about the prospect of military service. When the question on national service was followed by one asking teens if they would prefer military or non-military work, just 24% said they would prefer military work, while 75% would choose non-military work.

Responses to this question vary by gender; just 11% of girls said they would like military work, compared with 36% of boys. Eighty-eight percent of girls and 63% of boys would prefer non-military work.

Political Divide?

The political divide over the war in Iraq raises another question: Does the orientation of young people toward national service have a political tilt? Both leading presidential candidates, George W. Bush and John Kerry, encourage national service on a voluntary basis. Kerry in particular targets young people with his "Service for College" initiative, in which he promises four years of public university tuition in exchange for "two years in one of America's toughest and most important jobs," such as helping educate children in troubled schools or helping improve homeland security.

With regard to the general idea of a national service requirement, support is roughly equal among teens who said they plan to vote Republican when they are old enough and those who said they plan to vote Democratic: 40% of future Republicans supported the idea, as did 37% of future Democrats (support among those who said they will be political independents was slightly higher, at 48%). However, teens who plan to vote Republican were more likely to prefer military to non-military service: 42% said they'd rather serve in the military, compared with 17% of both future Democrats and independents.

IV. Community Service Programs

Editor's Introduction

During his 2002 State of the Union address, President George W. Bush called for the expansion of AmeriCorps and promised the organization an increase in funding. Bush also asked all Americans to dedicate 4,000 hours—roughly two years of their lives—to the national service program of their choice. Prior to that moment, Republicans had historically shown considerable skepticism about government-funded volunteer organizations. When President Bill Clinton founded AmeriCorps in 1993, for example, conservatives and libertarians rallied against him, contending that such a program would be pointless, as significant numbers of Americans volunteer on their own, without the help of any government-assisted program. An article by James Bovard in the conservative *American Spectator* derided AmeriCorps as a "scam" that operates "like a federal relief program for nightclub comics." The debate over AmeriCorps in many ways reflects a decades-long argument over government spending on volunteer programs. In this chapter, the first several entries examine the volunteer programs themselves, while the subsequent articles consider the debate over the government funding of such initiatives.

David Tarrant, in "Desire to Serve Stays for AmeriCorps Alums—Study," discusses the benefits of AmeriCorps, both for the communities served and the volunteers themselves. The article illustrates the profound impact volunteer work has had on countless lives and how AmeriCorps alumni have shown "a greater sense of civic responsibility and were more likely to remain involved in their communities than if they had not served."

"AmeriCorps Steps Up, Digs In," by Ken Leiser, further explores the positive impact the program has had, describing how AmeriCorps volunteers have helped rebuild the Gulf Coast in the aftermath of Hurricane Katrina. Leiser also explores AmeriCorps' day-to-day operations, focusing particularly on efforts to revitalize impoverished neighborhoods, tutor children in poor school districts, and other acts of volunteerism.

John Faherty discusses the Peace Corps in the subsequent article, "Peace Corps Finds Renewed Passion in Volunteerism." Steven Cole, a Peace Corps recruiter, described to Faherty the sort of qualities that are needed to excel as a volunteer. "The first thing is a global awareness," Cole remarked. "And a zeal, a passion, to understand another culture. If you don't have that, it doesn't matter how rugged you are, how much you want to help."

"How UN Volunteer System Assists" describes the United Nations' Volunteer Program and gives an overview of how its international programs help developing nations. The article also describes the considerable sacrifices required of U.N. volunteers as well as the benefits they receive for their service.

"Do the Nation a Service" by Senator John McCain is an overt appeal both for volunteers and for added assistance to volunteer programs. McCain cites President Bush's comments from the 2002 State of the Union Address and describes how the president is not living up to them. McCain provides examples of volunteers who were unable to continue their work for AmeriCorps due to a lack of funding, observing that their "patriotism has been spurned by Washington. . . . They have kept faith with America. The president who called them, and the Congress that praises them, should keep faith with them."

In "Denial of Service," Julian Sanchez rebukes McCain's stance, criticizing AmeriCorps for wasting money and participating in disreputable business practices, including what has been described as "Enron-like" accounting. He also accuses AmeriCorps volunteers of doing mostly nonproductive "busywork." "If it weren't for AmeriCorps, after all," Sanchez writes, "young people might decide they're perfectly capable of giving back to their communities without the assistance or direction of the federal government."

The renowned author Dave Eggers provides an unabashed defense of AmeriCorps in "Muting the Call to Service." "AmeriCorps," he writes, "has become, for an entire generation, the model for service." He cites volunteers culled from "the broadest spectrum of race, ethnicity and economic background imaginable" and describes hard-working volunteers who continue to serve the program long after their initial commitment has concluded. Like McCain, Eggers criticizes President Bush for providing far less support for AmeriCorps than promised. "Must we note that the $100 million that could save AmeriCorps is less than one-tenth of what we spend in Iraq every week?" Eggers asks.

Desire to Serve Stays for AmeriCorps Alums—Study

Members of Program Likely to Have More Civic Responsibility

BY DAVID TARRANT
THE DALLAS MORNING NEWS, DECEMBER 21, 2004

Wearing a red headscarf and heavy sweat shirt on this chilly morning, Kate Donahue helped pack a shipping container with construction materials at a West Dallas loading dock.

It's quite a change of scenery for Donahue, a 22-year-old interior design major from upstate New York. But just four months into a yearlong assignment as an AmeriCorps volunteer with Habitat for Humanity, she is already thinking long term.

"I don't know what I'll do after this. But I foresee that wherever I end up, I'll always be a part of Habitat for Humanity."

Young people are increasingly volunteering, working as mentors and tutors, running after-school programs and building affordable homes. Now, a new study shows that there is a long-term payoff for pitching in.

The report found that former volunteers of AmeriCorps, the largest of the country's national service programs, showed a greater sense of civic responsibility and were more likely to remain involved in their communities than if they had not served. Encouraging public service was a key goal when AmeriCorps was launched 10 years ago as a domestic version of the Peace Corps.

"Early findings of what will be a decades-long study show a strong and direct link between AmeriCorps membership and civic engagement later in life," said David Eisner, head of the Corporation for National and Community Service. "Service programs are important contributors to the long-term civic health of our nation."

The five-year study, commissioned by the federal corporation and conducted by Abt Associates, an independent social policy and research firm, tracked 2,000 AmeriCorps members since 1998, comparing them with an equal number of people who had inquired about the program but decided not to enroll. AmeriCorps members were significantly more likely to enter careers in public service such as teaching, public safety, social work and military service, the study reported.

Article by David Tarrant from *The Dallas Morning News*, December 21, 2004. Copyright © *The Dallas Morning News*. Reprinted with permission.

More than 380,000 men and women, mostly young people in their 20s, have served in AmeriCorps since the program started 10 years ago. Participation increased dramatically in 2004 to 75,000 volunteers—the largest class in its 10-year history—from 50,000 in 2003.

> *AmeriCorps has quietly become a major lure for recent college graduates with an altruistic bent.*

The 50 percent boost came after Congress gave the agency a $444 million budget in fiscal 2004, which included a record $170 million increase. The action represented a vote of confidence for the agency, after financial and management problems prompted criticism in Congress and forced management changes.

"Today, I won't say those problems are a distant memory—but it's safe to say they are in the rear-view mirror," said Eisner, a former vice president at AOL Time Warner, who took over the office last year.

In addition to AmeriCorps, the agency oversees the Senior Corps and Learn and Serve America programs.

AmeriCorps has quietly become a major lure for recent college graduates with an altruistic bent. The better-known Peace Corps, by contrast, only draws about 3,500 recruits annually with about 7,000 participants at any given time serving two-year commitments.

"It's popular and been popular all along," said Sandy Scott, spokesman for the Corporation for National & Community Service.

AmeriCorps volunteers sign up to work for 1,700 hours a year, mostly through community-based nonprofit programs. Volunteers receive a living stipend of about $10,000 a year, and upon completion of their service they are eligible for an education grant of $4,725.

Many students entering college already have volunteer experience, because increasingly high schools obligate students to perform community service.

The American Freshman survey, an annual study of more than 250,000 college freshman conducted by UCLA's Higher Education Research Institute, found this year that 83 percent of students reported "frequent or occasional volunteer work."

The trend contradicts the perception of young people as "slackers," with little or no interest in their communities or public issues.

"I can definitely attest to that," said Susan Weddington, president and chief executive officer of OneStar National Service Commission, which administers the federal AmeriCorps volunteer program for the state of Texas. About 1,200 AmeriCorps volunteers work in Texas, with at least 200 more expected by the end of February.

"What I see and experience is just the opposite—a real heightened sensitivity and sense of community," she said. "It's great to see."

The big beneficiary of this trend will be the nonprofit sector, said Weddington, who recalled one woman who was an anthropology major but decided on a career in nonprofit management after working as an AmeriCorps volunteer.

Pursuing a career with nonprofits is looking more interesting to Sarah Bellak, another AmeriCorps volunteer who works for Habitat for Humanity in Dallas.

Bellak, 22, of Indiana, Pa., had already been involved in a lot of church mission work in high school by the time she went to Juniata College in Huntingdon, Pa. "It's always been fun for me."

But more and more she sees value and meaning in what she's doing.

"It's exciting to see the walls go up and a family moving in," she said. "I'm realizing that I like this kind of work and could see doing it well into the future."

AmeriCorps Steps Up, Digs In

BY KEN LEISER
ST. LOUIS POST-DISPATCH (MISSOURI), JANUARY 23, 2006

Elzela Williams has seen snapshots of this coastal town [Pass Christian, Mississippi] taken before Hurricane Katrina delivered her knockout blow.

"It looked like paradise," said Williams, 41, of Jennings. "Far from it now."

Surging Gulf waters destroyed many of its picturesque, beachfront homes and ate away part of the white, sandy beach. Three-quarters of the homes were destroyed or damaged beyond repair. Businesses representing 98 percent of the town's tax base are gone.

Williams and other members of the St. Louis–based AmeriCorps emergency response team are helping this town get back on its feet—in ways large and small. No stranger to disasters, the team will remain in Pass Christian for at least the first year of its recovery.

The team's work is part of the effort launched last fall by the Corporation for National and Community Service—which oversees AmeriCorps—along with the Salvation Army and ABC-TV to assist in the reconstruction.

The AmeriCorps team recruits volunteers and puts them to work, clearing fallen trees, gutting houses and pitching in at the temporary town hall. On Friday, Williams' group chopped up tree trunks and branches near a town cemetery.

Josh Lewis, 27, of St. Louis, and others help out around "The Village," a tent city that houses some 140 Pass Christian residents. That includes furnishing the makeshift community center and fixing drainage around the green tents built by Navy Seabees.

"Personally, I am in charge of maintenance for this village back here—just making sure everything works," Lewis said. "These are people waiting for their FEMA trailers, displaced from their homes. They have nowhere to live right now."

Another project involves putting up stenciled street signs throughout town. The signs are important particularly after bulldozers roll in to scrape away storm-damaged homes, said Adam Rose, 23, of La Moille, Ill., a spokesman for the AmeriCorps disaster team.

"Had it not been for groups like AmeriCorps and Campus Crusade (for Christ), we couldn't have made it," said the city's Chief Administrative Officer Malcolm Jones. "The government has been good as

---

Reprinted with permission of the *St. Louis Post-Dispatch*, copyright © 2006.

far as providing technical assistance and funding. But there are times when we just need people . . . folks who can go out and do the work."

Public Safety, Education

Based in Soulard, the nonprofit AmeriCorps St. Louis started in the summer of 1994, making it one of the oldest AmeriCorps programs in the country, said Executive Director Bruce Bailey.

The group worked with St. Louis police and public schools to address public safety and education concerns in the city. To this day, AmeriCorps members mentor and tutor students in the St. Louis Public Schools.

In its first year of operation, AmeriCorps St. Louis responded to flooding in eastern Missouri and the 1995 bombing of the Alfred P. Murrah Federal Building in Oklahoma City, Bailey said. Since then the emergency response team has helped out in 29 states.

"In the early years, we operated very much like a volunteer fire department," Bailey said. "When there was a significant problem, we were asked to respond to round up people with special training and go do what was needed."

Out of that grew a special unit that, Bailey said, is one of a kind within AmeriCorps—a national service organization often thought of as a domestic Peace Corps. There are 40 people on the emergency response team right now. Twelve are in Pass Christian.

Full-time participants in AmeriCorps receive a living allowance, health insurance and a $4,725 education award after serving 10- to 12-month terms. Some members of the St. Louis team said last week that they had signed up for a second year.

After Katrina, the team moved into Jackson, Miss., and later fanned out to several hot spots through the Gulf Coast. The team helped the state of Mississippi set up a hot line for people who wanted to help out and a warehouse for donated goods.

"That team came in and became the backbone of that whole operation," said Marsha Kelly, director of the Mississippi Commission for Volunteer Service.

In Pass Christian, the group oversaw 270 volunteers who logged more than 10,000 service hours between Dec. 20 and Jan. 2.

> *Full-time participants in Ameri-Corps receive a living allowance, health insurance and a $4,725 education award after serving 10- to 12-month terms.*

Picking Up the Pieces

Nearly 7,000 people lived in Pass Christian before Katrina hit in late August. People drove from all over to snap pictures of the historic homes facing the Gulf, said Mayor Billy McDonald. Kelly likened it to Carmel, Calif., for its charm and beauty.

Until Katrina, Hurricane Camille of 1969 was the yardstick by which locals judged nature's fury. No more.

The surging Gulf of Mexico rose quickly by nearly 30 feet that morning, forcing people to scurry for their lives and trapping several police officers in the city library before they escaped—barely. Wind blew at 145 mph.

Although official figures are still elusive, City Administrator Jones said the death toll could reach more than 30. Some people are still missing, but many are surfacing—alive—in other parts of the country, Jones said.

The city lost the very equipment it would need to recover—backhoes, tractors, dump trucks.

But it's picking up the pieces, literally, with the help of the St. Louis team. In many places, residents are living in trailers provided by the Federal Emergency Management Agency. Trailers also house a restaurant, convenience store and bank near the tent city.

Jerry Lawson, a harbor patrol officer for the city, said he had called on AmeriCorps to help him clean up debris near the harbor.

"They sent about 20 people down, and those kids came out of those vans and cars and immediately started working," Lawson said. "You couldn't hire anybody to work as hard as they worked."

Williams worked at Lambert Field for 15 years as a driver for an airline catering company, and first thought about joining the Peace Corps instead of following his job to Chicago. He joined AmeriCorps nearly 1½ years ago and hasn't looked back.

"I always felt I made the right choice," he said while giving his chainsaw a break on Friday. "This is, again, what I was led to do."

Peace Corps Finds Renewed Passion in Volunteerism

By John Faherty
The Arizona Republic, October 21, 2005

The graphic images of people suffering in the wake of last year's tsunami and the rising casualties from the AIDS epidemic in Africa are spurring young people to get involved.

Today, the Peace Corps has more volunteers in the field than any time in the past 30 years. Of the 7,810 volunteers, 136 are from Arizona.

Joining means going to a developing country for 27 months to help locals live a better life.

The reasons for the renewed spirit of volunteerism are many and include:

- Increased global awareness after 9/11.

- Institutionalized volunteerism at many high schools.

- Support from the Bush administration to promote volunteerism, including active support of the Peace Corps.

"The world gets smaller and smaller all the time," said Sarah Daniels of Tucson.

Daniels spent two years in the Peace Corps in Namibia in Southwest Africa.

"I wanted to do something to help people, and this was a good way to do it," said Daniels, 28, who is now in her last year of medical school at the University of Arizona.

And there are many more people like her.

"People are caring more about things going on around the world," said David Briery, who works for the Peace Corps' Western region, which includes Arizona and Southern California. "I have a renewed faith in young people and what they seem to care about."

Desire to Help

Steven Cole is the Peace Corps recruiter at UA as well as an anthropology doctoral student. Last year, UA had 49 alumni serving in the corps.

He served two years in Zambia working with local people in agriculture and health programs. The experience was so rewarding he decided to serve another two years.

Article by John Faherty from *The Arizona Republic* October 21, 2005. Copyright © *The Arizona Republic*. Reprinted with permission.

When he talks to people who are thinking about joining, he tries to make sure they understand the commitment.

"The first thing is a global awareness," Cole said. "And a zeal, a passion, to understand another culture. If you don't have that, it doesn't matter how rugged you are, how much you want to help."

Cole knows it is a cliché about planting a seed of helping others when people are young, but it works.

Many high schools now have a community service program that ensures student involvement.

"The more you are exposed to volunteerism as a young person, the more likely you are to do something like the Peace Corps," Cole said. "I've had a lot of people who have referenced a high school teacher who put the idea of volunteerism in their head."

Peace Corp volunteers are provided with an allowance that lets them live similarly to the people in their community.

At the end of service, they receive $6,075 to help transition back to home.

Jacob Dang, 25, grew up in Mesa and is thinking about joining, despite his career as an engineer.

The face of the Peace Corp volunteer is changing.

The time commitment, more than two years, is giving him pause, but he still feels a desire to serve.

Dang is interested in "helping the unfortunate" and getting to see the world.

He is motivated, in part, by the fact that he knows he grew up more comfortably than most people.

His parents knew hardship before they emigrated from Vietnam. "I feel very fortunate, helping would be good," he said.

Eric Chase, 29, has been in Kenya for three months with the Peace Corps. He will work as a teacher.

His mother, Gail Chase of Phoenix, has been able to speak with him just once since he left.

"I am extremely proud of him," Gail said. "I'm happy for him, too, because this is such an adventure."

Gail said her son, a graduate of Bourgade Catholic High School in Phoenix, has always been aware of a bigger world beyond the borders of the United States.

"He has a social streak in him," she said. "He truly wants to make an impact on the world. Make things a little bit better, even if it is just in one village in Kenya."

Diversifying Volunteers

The face of the Peace Corp volunteer is changing. The average volunteer is now 28, and 6 percent of all volunteers are over 50.

The Peace Corps has also made a concerted effort to increase minority involvement, and now nearly one in six volunteers is a minority.

Briery says some people may be joining because of the president's encouragement.

"There has been a push with this administration for volunteerism in general. And for more Peace Corps volunteers," Briery said.

Gail Chase worried about her son when he first went to Kenya. "At first I was really concerned. Concerned about him getting sick, about all the cultural differences. . . . But he is doing great."

By the Numbers

Total volunteers, 2005: 7,810.

Arizonans: 136.

Gender by percent: 58 female, 42 male.

Minorities: 16 percent.

Over age 50: 6 percent.

Average age: 28.

Median age: 25.

Source: Peace Corps

How UN Volunteer System Assists Kenya

By Peter Mwaura
Daily Nation, March 12, 2003

On an average day, two or more applications from Kenyans are processed in Nairobi for voluntary work in development co-operation.

When I visited the United Nations Volunteer (UNV) Programme Office at Gigiri, one excited and exuberant middle-aged Kenyan woman was being assisted for a voluntary position in the Sudan.

A young man waited patiently on the side with his CV, possibly for posting to far-away Afghanistan or East Timor.

The UNV Office is building up a computerised roster of local applicants with a university degree and at least three years of experience in any field and would like to work in Kenya or abroad. The general duration of a UNV service contract is two years, renewable for eight years.

The Gigiri Office is a clearing-house. How quickly an applicant gets assigned depends on the client UN agency. An assignment could come in 10 days or 10 months.

Those recruited tend to fall between the ages of 25 and 75, with the majority having at least five years' working experience. Most Kenyan applicants tend be in their early 30s, have a master's degree and some 10 years' experience.

Those recruited are well-trained and experienced people who can hold their own in the international job market. They qualify for professional appointment with the United Nations system at middle-level grades.

Another class of volunteers is known as short-term advisory resources (UNISTAR) volunteers. These are highly qualified and successful people in their field of expertise. They include university professors, engineers, financial managers, consultants, manufacturing and marketing experts.

UNVs are not paid a salary. Instead they are given a living allowance of Sh49,400 for a citizen working in Kenya and between $1,562 and $1,993 for those working outside as internationals, depending on the country and the number of dependants.

Article by Peter Mwaura from *Daily Nation*, March 12, 2003. Copyright © Nation Media Group, Limited. Reprinted with permission.

According to Colette Ramm, the UNV Programme Co-ordinator for Kenya, some Kenyans seem to look upon the living allowance as a salary. This, she says, tends to be detrimental to the spirit of volunteerism.

In all, it costs the United Nations $15,000 a year to engage one national volunteer and $56,000 to engage one international UNV.

According to Ramm, UNVs provide flexibility and cost-effectiveness in the use of resources and their services should be used more.

> *The world is more than ever before turning to volunteers to solve the growing development problems of our times.*

The Kenya Government itself is using the services of UNVs in a number of areas, including poverty. During the last elections, some 200 UNV were fielded to support the electoral process.

In the past 20 years, more than 100 UNVs have worked in Kenya and today about 60 work in various parts of the country—from Turkana and Kakuma to Makueni and Kajiado, from Bungoma and Bondo to Garissa and Kilifi.

About one third of these volunteers are foreigners, the rest Kenyans—all working on various development projects, including good governance, HIV/Aids, gender and environmental issues. Kenya has one of the largest UNV programmes in Africa.

Worldwide, UNVs are the thousands. By the end of 2000, there were more than 20,000 professionals who had served or were still serving as UNVs in various countries.

Today volunteerism has become important in the area of development co-operation, and the United Nations is at the nerve centre of this worldwide phenomenon. Development co-operation is no longer seen as just dispatching highly paid experts, or funding ambitious development projects. It is increasingly being seen as relying on the commitment of qualified volunteers for whom financial rewards are not a primary consideration.

And the world is more than ever before turning to volunteers to solve the growing development problems of our times.

Volunteers take development to the people—they bring the UN to communities. When the UN General Assembly declared 2001 as the Year of Volunteers, Secretary-General Kofi Annan stated at the launch of the observance that volunteerism is "the ultimate expression of what the United Nations is all about."

Volunteerism is now recognised as a valuable, cross-cutting phenomenon. In December, 2001, the UN General Assembly devoted two plenary meetings to it.

It is hardly surprising that people who volunteer end up developing their own potentialities and career opportunities to a very high level.

For years, for example, Mr. Annan worked as a volunteer on the board of trustees of the United Nations School in New York before ascending to the position of UN Secretary-General. Mark Malloch Brown, the UNDP administrator, was a UN volunteer 25 years ago.

Gro Harlem Brundtland, director-General of the World Health Organisation, worked as a volunteer building a centre for the mentally handicapped. Ms. Carol Bellamy, executive director of Unicef, worked as a Peace Corps volunteer from 1963 to 1965 in Guatemala.

There are many other UN personalities who gained opportunities for career development through volunteerism. They include Thoraya Ahmed Obaid, executive director of the United Nations Population Fund; Ruud Lubbers, United Nations High Commissioner for Refugees; Juan Somavia, director-general for the ILO; Koichiro Matsuura, director-general of Unesco; and Noyleen Heyzer, executive director of the United Nations Fund for Women.

Sharon Capeling-Alakija, executive co-ordinator of the UNVs says that throughout her life as a volunteer and career working with volunteers: "I have never met a volunteer who didn't say they got more than they gave."

Do the Nation a Service

By John McCain
Newsweek, September 15, 2003

The attacks of September 11, for all the terrible suffering they caused, did have one good effect. For a time, they encouraged Americans to remember that as citizens of this good and great country we have responsibilities as well as rights that require our attention.

More than any time in recent years, Americans were unified not just in appreciation for our founding political convictions and the opportunities, prosperity and happiness they engender, but for patriotism that asks more of us than symbolic gestures of allegiance. We remembered that we are part of a cause greater than our individual self-interest, to which we, too, should proudly offer our services. And many Americans looked to their political leaders to welcome and help facilitate their desire for greater civic engagement.

Recognizing this, President Bush, in his 2002 State of the Union address, summoned Americans to serve causes "larger than self." He asked Americans to dedicate a total of two years of their lives to public service. He announced the establishment of a cabinet-level USA Freedom Corps Council to oversee the work of the government's volunteer programs. He promised to double the size of the Peace Corps, and to increase AmeriCorps, the government's principal domestic-service program, by 50 percent. Since then, the president has often paid eloquent tribute to volunteers in the dozens of community and national-service programs that AmeriCorps supports. As well he should.

Those programs, which range from tutoring at-risk kids to building homes for low-income families to fighting forest fires to homeland-security projects, involve Americans of all ages, ethnicity and backgrounds. They are a credit to our country, and the best assurance that the cynicism about public causes, about the very notion of citizenship, that afflicted some Americans in recent times, especially younger Americans, crested before September 11 and does not threaten the continued progress of this nation.

Yet, since the president first promised to expand opportunities for national service nearly two years ago, I've detected little effort by his administration to persuade Congress to provide funds for the plan. The administration has withheld support for legislation

---

Article by John McCain from *Newsweek*, September 15, 2003. Copyright © 2003. Reprinted with permission from John McCain.

that Sen. Evan Bayh and I introduced to increase AmeriCorps. We did win administration approval for a plan to encourage short-term enlistments in the military in exchange for education benefits, and to begin funding national-service programs that help communities with their homeland-security challenges. But beyond this modest support, his administration has neglected to match the president's rhetoric with concrete steps to keep his promise.

Most disappointing has been administration silence that amounts to tacit approval for the House Republican leadership's opposition to stopgap funding to help AmeriCorps keep operating at current levels. Due to the fiscal mismanagement of administration officials who ran the government corporation that oversees AmeriCorps, who accepted 20,000 new volunteers without adequate funds to support them, the program faces devastating cuts in its programs. The Senate, by a large majority, quickly appropriated $100 million to meet the shortfall, and new financial controls as well as new management were put in place to prevent the recurrence of sloppy accounting errors. But the House leadership refused to go along, and the White House acquiesced to their opposition. Thus, AmeriCorps has been forced to cut funding for nearly half its programs.

This discouraging lack of good faith means that Candace Spiller, a 19-year-old single mother, can no longer tutor poor children in the Mississippi Delta; Abraham Talbert, a high-school dropout who earned his GED and planned to go to college, will no longer build affordable housing for families in East Harlem, nor go to college, and Don Bullard, a disabled young man with a large heart, will no longer help other disabled Americans become self-reliant and valued members of their communities. These are three of the many thousands of volunteers whose patriotism has been spurned by Washington.

These good Americans have learned that serving a cause larger than themselves is as vital to their self-respect as it is useful to our country. They have kept faith with America. The president who called them, and the Congress that praises them, should keep faith with them.

Denial of Service

BY JULIAN SANCHEZ
REASON, OCTOBER 2003

"Enemies will use any weapon at their disposal" warned Sen. John McCain (R-Ariz.), in their ideological "attack on things that we believe in."

The senator was referring not to Ba'athist hard-liners but to the insidious congressional opponents of AmeriCorps. The Clinton-spawned Works Progress Administration for the new millennium was denied $100 million in emergency funding by a narrow House vote just before the August recess.

A spate of articles, including a *New York Times* op-ed by literary establishment darling Dave Eggers, quickly condemned such stinginess. Listening to these complaints, you might think the AmeriCorps budget had actually been cut. The reality is slightly more complex.

It turns out AmeriCorps' parent corporation had violated federal law by approving 20,000 more volunteers—and scholarships—than Congress had funded, spending $64 million it didn't have. The causes of this snafu included "little or no communication among key Corporation executives, too much flexibility given to grantees regarding enrollments, and unreliable data on the number of AmeriCorps participants," according to the General Accounting Office (GAO).

Despite what one Office of Management and Budget spokesman called "Enron-like" accounting, Congress increased AmeriCorps funding by $42 million in 2003. So how can activists at SaveAmericorps.org say that "Congress cut funding from $240 million to $175 million in Federal Fiscal Year 2003"? The misleading $175 million figure includes only the budget line item for grants and ignores appropriations for, among other things, a trust to help pay off that illegal debt.

The fiscal year 2004 appropriation raises AmeriCorps' budget by another 10 percent, but until that money kicks in, officials say it will be unable to fill 20,000 of its 50,000 volunteer slots without an emergency appropriation. Let's put this "drastic," "crippling" reduction in perspective.

Assume, implausibly, that every one of those 20,000 workers is a fulltime volunteer who completes the full 1,700 hours of AmeriCorps service, instead of bailing or being fired after resources have

---

Article by Julian Sanchez from *Reason*, October 2003. Copyright © *Reason*. Reprinted with permission.

already been spent training him, as was the case for a median of 39 percent of volunteers across 24 AmeriCorps programs the GAO examined in 1997. Assume that all of them are deterred from volunteering by the absence of AmeriCorps funds, even though some are teachers or teaching assistants who draw an independent salary. The Bureau of Labor Statistics reported that in the past year 59 million Americans volunteered a mean 143 hours each; other surveys put the figure even higher. The AmeriCorps cuts then represent about four-tenths of 1 percent of total American volunteer hours.

This is not a deadweight loss. AmeriCorps pays some volunteers who'd probably do at least some work for free. It also diverts private and state funds to programs that bear its imprimatur.

What sort of programs? Well, McCain, who hopes AmeriCorps will encourage participants to become politically involved, seems to be getting his wish. In 1995 it gave a $1.1 million grant to the Association of Community Organizations for Reform Now, a group whose activities include lobbying for "living wages" and subsidized low-income housing. (The grant eventually had to be returned.) Teachers and tutors undergo sensitivity training in which they identify themselves as economic, racial, and religious "oppressors" or "oppressed." AmeriCorps volunteers have also done busywork for a variety of federal agencies and bought toy guns back from toddlers.

AmeriCorps volunteers do accomplish some genuine good. But like the "national greatness" conservatives, many AmeriCorps boosters seem more interested in the grand sense of national community the program is meant to inspire. If it weren't for AmeriCorps, after all, young people might decide they're perfectly capable of giving back to their communities without the assistance or direction of the federal government. And wouldn't that be a tragedy?

Muting the Call to Service

BY DAVE EGGERS
THE NEW YORK TIMES, AUGUST 2, 2003

    A little over a week ago, in New Orleans, I met two young women who had driven hours, through the heat of July, in rural Louisiana, to talk to me about tutoring kids. Sarah Garb and Megan Peterson are both in their early 20's, both graduates of very good colleges, and both have been living in Clinton, a tiny Louisiana town far from any large city, a town with quite literally one stoplight. They were Teach for America participants who had committed two years of their lives to teaching in low-performing schools. After they talked with me and a pair of men who run a tutoring center through Tulane University, it was 11 p.m., and time for them to drive back.

    I just finished a tour where I spoke to would-be volunteers in nine cities about the number of public school students who can use their help and spare time, in whatever quantities, for tutoring and mentoring. Eighteen months ago, a few friends and I started a non-profit afterschool tutoring program in San Francisco called 826 Valencia. Our goal was to make it easy for volunteers to help students between the ages of 8 and 18 with their English and writing skills. Because we're flexible about volunteers' time commitments and because the teachers of San Francisco are burdened with ever-increasing class sizes and diminished resources, we've been overflowing with volunteers and our programs are growing every month. The need is there, and people want to help.

    But Sarah Garb and Megan Peterson, the two teachers from Clinton, went much further than just helping out in their spare time, as the volunteers at 826 Valencia do. When I met them, they were not what one would think of as born crusaders, and they certainly didn't grow up thinking they would one day be teaching in rural Louisiana. They looked very much like two people who might be living in Lincoln Park in Chicago, or the Upper East Side, or the Marina District in San Francisco, enjoying considerably more comfortable lives. But instead they were far from all of that, struggling every day, earning just above minimum wage, and every day making a huge difference in the lives of the fifth and sixth graders whom they were teaching. And more remarkably, they had chosen to stay. That is, after their two-year commitment expired in June, they made arrangements with the school district to stay, perhaps indefinitely, in Clinton.

Copyright © 2003 by The New York Times Co. Reprinted with permission.

The power of Teach for America is that it can redirect lives, it can make bright young people aware of where they're most needed and where they'll find the most rewarding work. This is why we need Teach for America, and why we need AmeriCorps, the national service program that helps finance Teach for America and other initiatives (Habitat for Humanity and Save the Children, for example). AmeriCorps gives annual grants to 50,000 volunteers, who serve up to a year and receive an award of $4,725 toward higher education as well as a modest living allowance. Last year, AmeriCorps made it possible to bring thousands of full-time teachers to hundreds of schools, from New Mexico's Navajo Nation to the District of Columbia.

> *AmeriCorps—and the initiatives it supports—has become, for an entire generation, the model for service.*

And lest you consider AmeriCorps a program made up of wealthy white college graduates padding their résumés: I recently visited the San Jose, Calif., chapter of City Year, another AmeriCorps-sponsored program. Here, volunteers help in schools, run theater workshops and provide afterschool programs during the week and learning programs for middle and high school students on the weekends. The volunteers I met represented the broadest spectrum of race, ethnicity and economic background imaginable. There was a 20-year-old single mother trying to raise two children on an AmeriCorps stipend and a 19-year-old Princeton-bound volunteer from Las Vegas. They were an inspiring group—all energized, all ready to do what they were called upon to do, all even wearing matching uniforms—white shirts, tan shorts.

AmeriCorps—and the initiatives it supports—has become, for an entire generation, the model for service. But unless something is done very soon, the number of AmeriCorps participants will be slashed by as much as 50 percent in the next few months. Five of the 13 City Year programs will be forced to shut down, leaving tens of thousands of students around the country without the benefit of its tutoring, mentoring and literacy efforts.

AmeriCorps needs an emergency infusion of $100 million just to maintain its current operations. While the Senate voted to appropriate the money, the House of Representatives refused to approve the emergency funds—and then adjourned for the summer. Meanwhile, the administration has been largely silent—and it remains unclear whether it will press Congress to provide the funds in September.

Which is confusing, considering how vocal President Bush has been about the need to maintain and even expand our national service programs. At one time, in fact, the president proposed expanding AmeriCorps to 75,000 members. "We need more talented teachers in troubled schools," the president said in his 2002 State of the Union address, the first after 9/11. "U.S.A. Freedom Corps will expand and improve the good efforts of AmeriCorps and Senior Corps to recruit more than 200,000 new volunteers."

It was the president's words that encouraged young people to send in AmeriCorps applications. Thousands of outrageously qualified applicants were prepared to quit high-paying jobs, to put off graduate school, to move to, say, rural Louisiana—all in the name of national service, in the name of doing something selfless for a country that needed healing. AmeriCorps approved new volunteer slots and assumed it had the support of Congress and the president. Now, on the eve of a new school year, Congress and the White House have turned their backs on these volunteers.

Must we note that the $100 million that could save AmeriCorps is less than one-tenth of what we spend in Iraq every week? Is it too obvious to mention that the president, who long scorned nation-building abroad while encouraging education here at home, is now clearly choosing the former over the latter?

It's no secret that many in the G.O.P. have long favored the dissolution of AmeriCorps. And though the process won't necessarily be speedy, Republicans in the House are well on their way to making the program a thing of the past. And what happens then? Who or what steps into the chasm created by the White House's failure to act? No one knows. But what is certain is that a generation that was beginning to engage with government, with citizenship and service, will be abandoned, and will be given good reason to shrug back into an easy and familiar, "Well, what did you expect?" sort of cynicism. In fact, the best and most idealistic members of this generation are the ones who will feel most betrayed. Preventing this is within Washington's power—and $100 million is, relatively speaking, a paltry amount to pay for keeping alive the volunteer spirit of the youth of this country.

V. Mandatory Universal National Service

Editor's Introduction

"Our times have been dramatically altered by two defining events: the tragedy of Sept. 11 and Hurricane Katrina," Alan Khazei and Michael Brown observe in "Uncle Sam Wants You." Arguments for and against government-mandated, nonmilitary service programs are often placed in the context of these two seminal events. While a draft may indeed be far off, some public educational institutions have made community service a prerequisite for graduation. Though by no means a universal national service mandate, this is a clear example of the government's willingness to compel young people to volunteer and has stirred strong emotions.

Eric Slater, in "Monterey Bay Campus Is a Role Model," reports on California State University, whose Monterey Bay campus was, at the time of the article's writing, the only public institution of higher learning in California to make community service a requirement for graduation. Slater discusses the debate prompted by the policy and looks at what sort of community service programs the school offered and how they were relevant to the students' fields of study. The school's plan did draw some criticism: The *Los Angeles Times* printed a letter denouncing the program several days after the university announced the initiative. "The contention that one owes service to his community implies that the community owns his life," the letter read. "This is the essence of slavery. The purpose of mandatory community service programs in schools is to persuade students that self-interest is immoral. This is inconsistent with the American theory of government."

In "Kids with a Cause," Cathy Gulli describes similar volunteer programs for high school students, which are becoming increasingly common in Canada. Gulli quotes both advocates and opponents of the initiatives.

In "Uncle Sam Wants You," Alan Khazei and Michael Brown examine particular pieces of legislation that encouraged national service during the 20th century, citing various benefits awarded to veterans who served during World War II. "The most commonly asked question of an 18-year-old should be," according to the writers, "'Where will you do your citizen service? The Army or AmeriCorps? The Marines or the National Civilian Community Corps? The Navy or the Peace Corps?'" They argue that the U.S. "needs universal, voluntary national service[,] the expectation that everyone should serve and the opportunity for everyone to do so linked to a new GI Bill that dramatically changes the life prospects of those who serve in the military and those who serve in our neediest schools and neighborhoods."

Robert E. Litan echoes these sentiments in "September 11, 2001: The Case for Universal Service," in which he correlates the need for national security with a mandatory service program. "Unlike America's past foreign wars," he writes, "the war on terrorism requires a vigilant homeland security effort in addition to an offensive military (and intelligence) campaign abroad. . . . Young people in service, provided they were properly trained, could substantially augment the guards now in place at a wide range of public and private facilities." As an example, Litan cites American ports, where, "only a tiny fraction of incoming containers is examined." He also endorses national service, arguing that it provides a kind of "social glue" that could unite the nation's increasingly diverse populace.

In "A Bad Idea Whose Time Is Past: The Case Against Universal Service," Bruce Chapman offers a vivid contrast to Litan's piece. "Trying to justify universal service on moral grounds is also a mistake," Chapman writes. "Morally, service isn't service to the extent it is compelled. Involuntary voluntarism is like hot snow." Chapman also argues that a mandatory service program that proved to be unpopular might elicit an unpatriotic attitude from the nation's youth.

Drake Bennett provides a different anti-service argument in "Doing Disservice," contending that such programs divert attention from societal problems by providing solutions that can yield only short-term results. "Systematic government solutions rather than piecemeal acts of goodwill better address many of the problems that volunteers tackle," he observes. "If hospitals and libraries increasingly rely on volunteers, it's because reduced federal appropriations are starving institutions that depend on public funding. In this context, well-intentioned young people who fill the gap are enablers of the attack on public services."

The final article, Alan W. Dowd's "A Nation of Servants: Defining Public Service for the Twenty-first Century," serves as a counterpoint to the book's first article, by Harris Wofford. Dowd, like Wofford, discusses the history of national service programs, but where Wofford lobbies for such programs, Dowd is consistently critical of them. "After seventy years of federal service programs," he writes, "proponents of national service still complain that not enough Americans are serving and those who do aren't serving enough." Dowd argues that, "counteracting selfishness with service is indeed important. However, Washington does not need to pass new legislation, restart the draft, or create new programs to achieve that balance."

Monterey Bay Campus Is a Role Model

BY ERIC SLATER
LOS ANGELES TIMES, AUGUST 10, 2004

To graduate from college, Tracy Burke spent time in a halfway house for female felons. Alicia Gregory filled grocery bags at a food bank. Tiana Trutna taught elementary students how to grow vegetables for their school cafeteria.

Here at Cal State Monterey Bay, it's required work. To the university, it's an essential part of an education. But some educators elsewhere say required community service squanders precious education dollars—and time.

The only public university or college in the state to require such service, Monterey Bay is finding itself at the center of a fast-growing debate as California begins to consider whether to mandate community service for all 3.4 million students in the public system.

The notion that such service should be required for a college degree was among the many proposals to emerge last week from the California Performance Review, a report commissioned by Gov. Arnold Schwarzenegger that addresses hundreds of aspects of state government.

At issue, first, is whether it is appropriate to require community service as part of what goes into a university degree. Beyond that, even among those who support mandatory service, there is disagreement over how best to make such service meaningful.

Mandatory service might be of little value, some say, without accompanying academic study—"service learning," as it's known.

"Requiring community service is a good first step," said Stephen M. Reed, associate vice president for external relations at Monterey Bay. "But it's only a first step."

Students here not only must work in the community; they also must take courses related to that work.

"The important thing is not contributing hours," said Seth Pollack, director of the university's Service Learning Institute. "The important thing is learning your own responsibility to your community. That comes not from parking cars or licking envelopes, but from understanding the root causes of our social problems."

Article by Eric Slater from the *Los Angeles Times*, August 10, 2004. Copyright © *Los Angeles Times*. Reprinted with permission.

The state's colleges and universities have long urged their students to volunteer for good causes of all kinds, and hundreds of thousands of students do. The California Performance Review advocated taking such volunteerism a step further: converting voluntary service into mandatory community work for students.

All but hidden among the 50,000 acres of artillery ranges and deteriorating barracks of the now-defunct Ft. Ord Army base, Cal State Monterey Bay has been an outpost of civic-minded academics since the day it opened nine years ago, a place where theories of ethics, community and multiculturalism are debated while the military detonates aging munitions nearby.

In part because of its service requirement, the school has acquired a reputation as a left-leaning establishment, though the area also is known for military-style conservatism, thanks to Ft. Ord, the Naval Postgraduate School and other military installations.

The university's pioneers laid the groundwork for socially conscious scholarship in the school's vision statement, written in 1994, which pledges to imbue students with the "responsibility and skills to be community builders."

All students must take eight units of service-study courses—four while fulfilling their basic general education requirements and four related to their major, all while working in the community.

They have 40 such courses to choose from—everything from "Museum Studies Service Learning" to classes on tutoring in mathematics—and students are encouraged to explore a field they might otherwise never experience.

As a communications major from a white, middle-class family in the suburbs of San Francisco, Burke chose to work in a minimum-security facility in Salinas for female convicts with young children.

"I knew a couple of people in high school who had drug problems, but their parents had the money to send them to rehab," Burke said. "This was just this huge eye-opener—about how this happens, about how the society is shaped."

The recommendation of the governor's task force, complete with quotes from Gandhi and the governor's wife, Maria Shriver, is not the first time a service requirement has been recommended for all public universities. In 1999, Gov. Gray Davis floated a nearly identical proposal.

Thomas Sowell, a fellow at Stanford University's Hoover Institution, lambasted the notion then. "Forced to volunteer," he wrote of Democrat Davis' proposal, "is the Orwellian notion to which contemporary liberalism has sunk."

Sowell might have been among the more politically outspoken opponents, but he had lots of company—most notably all three branches of state higher education: the University of California system, the California State system and the state's community colleges.

None implemented Davis' recommendation. The reasons were many, but money was at the top of the list. Student labor is cheap only for the groups employing the students.

"It takes a tremendous amount of resources to properly administer these programs," said Season Eckhardt, Cal State's director of communications for service learning. "Before we would endorse a requirement, we would want to talk to a lot of people."

The Cal State and UC systems agreed earlier this year to expand their voluntary community service programs in a deal with Schwarzenegger that sets fee increases and funding levels for the next several years, even though Cal State had its service budget cut in half last year, to $1.1 million.

All three state systems have offices that help students who want to volunteer find community groups in need, as well as service learning courses in some academic disciplines. About one-third of UC's 200,000 students perform volunteer work, as do 45% of Cal State's more than 400,000 students, officials said.

What is clear is that all three systems have received the new panel's proposal with the same tepid response they gave Davis'

Student labor is cheap only for the groups employing the students.

---

plan, noting the cost and pointing out that the average age of community college students, for example, is 28—and many of them have children and full-time jobs.

"Community service is a very good thing," community college spokeswoman Cheryl Fong said, "but I think that we need to carefully look at whether it should be an institution-wide requirement."

Pollack, the director of Monterey Bay's service learning institute, says he was once a skeptic. But, the key, he insists, is to give students a strong academic foundation in social justice issues, race, poverty and ethics so that when they go out to help in the community, the experience can mean more than just checking off another graduation requirement.

Launching a university with this as a core value, officials here acknowledge, may be enormously simpler than instituting it at existing schools, many of them much larger.

The university here has nine faculty and staff members dedicated to the program, with a budget of $400,000 and $200,000 more in grant money.

Virtually every instructor and many staff members play a role, because every student on campus is involved. Many current and former students said they had been required to perform community service in high school and got little out of it besides the right to graduate.

"I think our governor needs to do some more research before taking a step in that direction," said 20-year-old junior Marissa Serma.

Studying drug addiction, Serma and several other students agreed, can make working with addicts educational; learning about the relationship of poverty to crime rates and the demographics of the prison population helps demystify those they meet at shelters and halfway houses.

When combined with academic study, service requirements become "like opera," said Gregory, 19, a junior theater major. "Even if you don't really like it, you can understand and appreciate it."

Kids with a Cause

By Cathy Gulli
Maclean's, November 21, 2005

Every Monday evening, Dushyandi Rajendran trades in her backpack and textbooks for another set of learning tools—coloured papers and a yellow smock. Once she's got her homework and supper out of the way, the Grade 12 student heads out to an unlikely night class essential for her to graduate next spring: Japanese paper-folding.

Seventeen-year-old Rajendran, who attends Marc Garneau Collegiate in Toronto, is putting in community service hours at Princess Margaret Hospital Lodge, an off-site facility for cancer patients. There, she helps teach a weekly origami class through the Canadian Cancer Society. But Rajendran insists she's the one benefiting most from these sessions. "Hearing people's stories and talking with them, I've learned so much about life experiences, and about what people have to live with," she says. "They have so much to offer, and it's such a great thing to see."

Forty hours of community service is compulsory for all Ontario high school students before graduation. But across the country, only five areas do the same—British Columbia and the Yukon (both 30 hours), and the Northwest Territories and Nunavut (25 hours). Newfoundland has introduced a pilot project among Grade 10 students mandating that they complete 30 hours of community service in order to graduate. This year, 45 of 130 high schools are participating, and in 2006 the requirement will be province-wide.

A recent study by the Catholic University of America in Washington, however, shows that forcing students to volunteer is in their best interests, and leads to more civic-minded, socially active adults. "If it's a good program," says James Youniss, who studied Boston high school students between 2000 and 2002, "and they're getting something meaningful out of it, then it's irrelevant if students were forced to do it."

And students almost always have a meaningful experience, says Bill Conconi, executive director of the Canadian Association of Student Activity Advisors, which promotes high school leadership programs. "Most kids have enjoyed the experience because even though it's compulsory, where they do it and how they do it is voluntary. There are all sorts of places to get experience." Whether students choose to entertain at a seniors' residence, serve as lifeguards at the local pool, or job-shadow a veterinarian, the benefits are the same. "It's a way of providing links to the larger community," says Helen Raham, research director for the Ottawa-based Society for the Advancement of Excellence in Education. "It should be a win-win, whereby the community benefits, and the student gains a lot of insight, empathy and skills."

In most cases, students also gain work experience. "Even from Day 1 it's not much different than if they were applying for a paid job," says Leslie Sheriff, volunteer resources coordinator at Princess Margaret lodge, adding that the students must comport themselves as if they were paid workers.

So with this many benefits to be gained from mandatory volunteerism, why aren't other jurisdictions introducing it? Forced volunteerism, some provinces say, requires resources most schools lack, and is contrary to the spirit of community service. And, notes Conconi, schools and volunteer organizations often worry about liability. "There is a certain concern that you're accepting some responsibilities that you may not want to have. It may be difficult to get good placements, and to make sure that [students] are put in a safe environment." Raham notes that an unwilling volunteer can be more hindrance than help to an organization. "I think the challenge is to find an area where the student is interested in volunteering. And that takes counselling, staff facilities to make those liaisons, and partnerships. Schools say they haven't got the resources."

With little Canadian cost-benefit research about mandatory community service, says Raham, few education ministries feel compelled to take on the added work. "On the face of it, this seems like a useful direction to go. But research would be helpful to support the general belief." For Rajendran, though, there's no question about the value of compulsory volunteerism. "If it wasn't required I don't know if I would be doing this," she says. "I don't think a lot of people would be."

Where They Can Help

While volunteering is mandatory for many high school students in Canada, they choose which service to do. The most common placements involve helping the homeless, sick or elderly, organizing school events, and job-shadowing (especially veterinarians).

Uncle Sam Wants You

By Alan Khazei and Michael Brown
The Boston Globe, December 7, 2005

Our times have been dramatically altered by two defining events: the tragedy of Sept. 11 and Hurricane Katrina.

A prescription for these times has roots in the nation's successful response to the crises of the last century. The GI Bill was an enormous success: Between 1945 and 1956, more than 8 million returning veterans received debt-free educations, low-interest mortgages, and small-business loans, making the United States, in the words of one historian, "the predominantly middle-class nation it had always believed itself to be."

It is time for a new call to service to meet the pressing needs of the nation, reinvigorate American citizenship, and provide access to the American dream.

Our nation needs universal, voluntary national service [,] the expectation that everyone should serve and the opportunity for everyone to do so linked to a new GI Bill that dramatically changes the life prospects of those who serve in the military and those who serve in our neediest schools and neighborhoods.

Service to the nation whether in the armed services or a civilian service corps should become a defining emblem of the United States and a civic rite of passage for all young Americans. The most commonly asked question of an 18-year-old should be: "Where will you do your citizen service? The Army or AmeriCorps? The Marines or the National Civilian Community Corps? The Navy or the Peace Corps?"

A new GI Bill could make this promise to every young American: "If you invest in your country, your country will invest in you. For every year you serve, America guarantees a year of tuition at a qualifying college, makes a down payment toward your first home, or provides a voucher to start a business, nonprofit organization, or IRA." Military service, which demands greater sacrifice, would garner higher benefits, but all who serve should be rewarded.

There is a new generation ready to build a stronger America. Recent research has shown that 9/11 was a transformational event for 18- to 24-year-olds: They have a significantly higher civic commitment. The tragedies of that day inspired a sharp increase in applications to the military, the Peace Corps, and AmeriCorps.

Article by Alan Khazei and Michael Brown from *The Boston Globe*, December 7, 2005. Copyright © *The Boston Globe*. Reprinted with permission.

Over 16 years, led by three successive presidents, America has built a strong civilian national service system, which is now ready to be brought to scale. George H.W. Bush established the Commission on National and Community Service and the Points of Light Foundation. Bill Clinton created the Corporation for National and Community Service and AmeriCorps. George W. Bush launched the USA Freedom Corps and expanded AmeriCorps and the Peace Corps.

National service has had a profound impact on America. AmeriCorps has enabled more than 400,000 citizens to serve with more than 2,500 nonprofit and faith-based organizations. These leaders have built affordable homes, helped thousands of children to read, provided millions of hours of after-school programs, reduced gang involvement, transformed blighted lots into community gardens and playgrounds, served as role models to children at risk, and generated millions of hours of service by the volunteers they recruit. A cost-benefit study of AmeriCorps determined that every federal dollar invested results in at least $1.60 to $2.60 in direct, measurable benefits. It is time for a dramatic increase in AmeriCorps, from 75,000 annually to 1 million strong, a domestic force against poverty and hopelessness.

> *Both military and civilian service provide young Americans with an opportunity to work side by side across lines of race and class.*

Around the world, over four decades, more than 175,000 Americans have served in the Peace Corps. However, the 7,700 currently in service are a far cry from President John F. Kennedy's vision of 100,000 "citizen ambassadors." It is time to reach that goal.

Both military and civilian service provide young Americans with an opportunity to work side by side across lines of race and class. Expanding and uniting military and civilian service under one GI Bill can further close the gap between military and civilian cultures. At its widest during the Vietnam War era, this gap has diminished since 9/11. It is time to close it altogether.

A system that unites military and civilian service, launched with a new "Uncle Sam wants you!" campaign, should offer one-stop recruitment centers in colleges, malls, neighborhood store fronts, and online. ROTC should be restored to all campuses and its mission expanded to prepare young leaders for military and civilian service. A US Civic Leadership Academy should develop civilian leaders just as the four major military academies prepare the leaders of our armed forces.

Every generation can be the "greatest generation" if only it is called to serve a cause larger than self. Nothing could be more American, or more invigorating to the very idea of America.

September 11, 2001

The Case for Universal Service

BY ROBERT E. LITAN
BROOKINGS REVIEW, FALL 2002

Americans are a generous people. The attacks of September 11 produced an outpouring of donations to help families of the victims. Americans took pride in the heroism of public servants—firefighters, the police, FBI agents, and men and women in the military—who responded to the call of duty. It was also widely felt that September 11 would change the lives of many young Americans, who not only would have the images of the attacks seared into their memories, but also would pursue careers in public service or the "helping" professions.

Time will tell whether those initial impulses toward helping others will last. But time alone won't determine the outcome. Public policy can and will have an impact. If Americans want more of their children to pursue service careers or at least devote time to activities that help and support others, whether in the public or private sector, it will certainly help if government encourages or provides opportunities for such service. The same is true for adults wishing to serve in some capacity, as many apparently were willing to do in the weeks following September 11.

President Bush, for one, has recognized the role of public policy by supporting a much-expanded voluntary national service program. In his fiscal year 2003 budget, he called for the creation of the USA Freedom Corps, which would combine and expand the Peace Corps and AmeriCorps programs and add a new Senior Corps as well as a volunteer program for college students. Bush proposed increasing the funding of all national service programs by nearly $300 million and eventually placing more than 2 million Americans a year in some kind of formal national service (75,000 in full-time AmeriCorps programs). He also called on Americans to give two years over the course of their lives to service.

The Bush proposals tap into two strong American traditions—a commitment to volunteerism and a resistance to compulsory service except in wars requiring a massive call-up. With the exception of some community service programs in some high schools in certain states, this nation has never required its young citizens to perform civilian service.

Article by Robert E. Litan from *Brookings Review*, Fall 2002. Copyright © *Brookings Review*. Reprinted with permission.

The president's call to service may be working. Applications by college graduates to AmeriCorps are up 75 percent and applications to the Peace Corps are up 18 percent, according to a June survey in *Time*. But the surge in interest may also be linked to the poor job market this past year for college graduates.

There are limits to volunteerism. Can we do more?

In short, there are limits to volunteerism. Can we do more? Here I lay out the case for moving beyond even the president's new initiative toward some kind of universal service requirement, one that would offer all young Americans a choice, preferably after finishing high school, to enter military or civilian service for at least a year. Those opting and qualifying for the military would be given additional monetary incentives to do so.

Having a reasoned debate about universal service before September 11 would have been unthinkable. It isn't (or at least shouldn't be) so anymore.

The Case for Universal Service, Now

As the Bush administration has reminded us, we are at war—this time, against an enemy whose main targets of attack are American civilians. Unlike past wars, this new war on terrorism, we are told, could last a generation or more. If, as appears likely, the nation may soon be at war with Iraq again, the question arises: why should the burden of the war—and the risks of getting injured or killed—rest only on the shoulders of those who volunteer to fight it?

There are answers to this question, of course. One is that the military should be able to handle even a stepped-up military campaign against terrorism. After all, the armed forces fought Iraq in 1991 with roughly 500,000 troops; this time around, the highest projections seem to fall in the 250,000 range. A second answer is that the men and women in uniform are paid to put themselves in harm's way, and they volunteered to assume any risk of war that may come about.

But unlike America's past foreign wars, the war on terrorism requires a vigilant homeland security effort in addition to an offensive military (and intelligence) campaign abroad. This time around, it is not just those in the military who are in harm's way. We are all potential targets or victims—and thus all have some obligation to help secure America. As a practical matter, neither the economy nor society could function if everyone stood guard duty or devoted their time to protecting the homeland. Paid professionals have and will continue to carry out these duties. But if this new war is as it is said to be, a generational event, then why not also ask the next generation—all of whom may be at risk—to help shoulder the security effort?

The need is there. Young people in service, provided they were properly trained, could substantially augment the guards now in place at a wide range of public and private facilities. The nation could also use many more inspectors at its ports—perhaps our greatest vulnerability today—where only a tiny fraction of incoming containers is examined. Some highly motivated young people may even decide to train for security-related careers—as police officers, customs or immigration officials, or FBI agents—and serving in all of these jobs should qualify for universal service.

Though one good reason for adopting universal service now is to respond to the military and homeland threat, universal service makes sense in other ways in this time of national peril.

First, universal service could provide some much-needed "social glue" in an embattled American society that is growing increasingly diverse—by race, national origin, and religious preference—and where many young Americans from well-to-do families grow up and go to school in hermetically sealed social environments. Twenty years ago, when America was much less diverse than it is now and is going to be, the editorial page of the *Wall Street Journal* (of all places) opined that mandatory service would constitute a "means for acculturation, acquainting young people with their fellow Americans of all different races, creeds, and economic backgrounds."

Those words are as compelling today as when they were written. A service program in which young people from different backgrounds work and live together would do far more than college ever could to immerse young Americans in the diversity of our country. It would also help sensitize more fortunate young men and women, at an impressionable point in their lives, to the concerns and experiences of others from different backgrounds and give them an enduring appreciation of what life is like "on the other side of the tracks."

Second, universal service could promote civic engagement, which, as Harvard social scientist Robert Putnam has persuasively argued in *Bowling Alone*, has been declining—or at least was before September 11. Some who perform service for the required period may believe their civic responsibilities will thereby be discharged, but many others are likely to develop an appreciation for helping others that could change the way they lead the rest of their lives.

Third, young people serving in a civilian capacity in particular would help satisfy unmet social needs beyond those associated with homeland security: improving the reading skills of tens of millions of Americans who cannot now read English at a high school level, cleaning up blighted neighborhoods, and helping provide social, medical, and other services to the elderly and to low-income individuals and families. Allowing individuals to delay their service until after college would enable them to bring skills to their service that could prove even more useful to society and may be a desirable option. But doing so would also reduce the benefits of added social cohesion from universal service, because it would tend to create two tiers of service, one for those who don't go to college and another for those who do.

Finally, universal service would establish firmly the notion that with rights for ourselves come responsibilities to others. Of course, the Constitution guarantees all citizens certain rights—of free speech, of due process of law, to be free from discrimination, to vote—without asking anything of them in return. But why shouldn't citizens be required to give something to their country in exchange for the full range of rights to which citizenship entitles them?

Countering the Objections

As Bruce Chapman makes clear in the article that follows, imposing a universal service requirement would raise serious objections aside from the philosophical one—opposition to any form of government compulsion and the temporary loss of liberty it entails.

Probably the most serious argument against universal service is its cost.

Probably the most serious argument against universal service is its cost. Roughly 4 million students graduate from high school each year. A good benchmark for costs is the AmeriCorps program. According to official figures, the federal government spent roughly $10,000 for each AmeriCorps volunteer in fiscal year 2001. A plausible assumption is that the states and the private sector added perhaps another $7,000 (according to a 1995 study by the General Accounting Office, these costs amounted then to about $5,500 per person, so they might be close to $7,000 now). Given the relatively small numbers enrolled in AmeriCorps—about 50,000 annually—its per person costs may be higher than those for a much larger universal program, which would be able to amortize overhead costs over a much larger population. On the other hand, not all AmeriCorps volunteers live in a dormitory setting. Providing dormitories for all participants in a universal civilian program would raise the cost relative to AmeriCorps.

Balancing these factors, I assume here for illustrative purposes a per person cost of $20,000, which, if funded entirely by the federal government, would bring the total annual gross cost of the entire program to about $80 billion. From this figure, it would be necessary to subtract the costs of those who already serve in AmeriCorps and the Peace Corps, as well as high school students who now volunteer for the military. In addition, some participants in a universal service program might be performing functions now carried out by paid workers. Taking all these offsets into account could bring the annual net incremental cost of the program down to, say, the $70 billion range—still a very large number.

Given the recent dramatic deterioration of the federal budget, a program of that magnitude would seem now to be a political nonstarter, and it may well be. Nonetheless, one potentially fair way to reduce costs and thereby make the idea of universal service more palatable from a budgetary perspective would be to implement the requirement initially as a lottery, much like the system that existed toward the end of the Vietnam War. Depending on the cut-off point, the program could be sized at any level that the political traffic could bear.

However large the program could turn out to be, those who may be tempted to dismiss as too costly a universal service requirement of any size must consider its benefits. A 1995 GAO cost-benefit analysis, for example, positively evaluated the findings of a 1995 study by George R. Neumann, Roger C. Kormendi, Robert F. Tamura, and Cyrus J. Gardner that had cited quantifiable monetary benefits of $1.68 to $2.58 for every dollar invested in three AmeriCorps programs. These estimates did not count the nonquantifiable, but very real, benefits of strengthening local communities and fostering civic responsibility. Nor did they include the broader benefits of added social cohesion that a universal program would entail. On the other side of the ledger, it is quite possible that there would be diminishing returns to a much broader program than AmeriCorps, and thus at some enrollment level the costs of a universal requirement could exceed the benefits. But even this result—which is hardly ensured—would not credit the nonquantifiable social benefits of a broader program.

The bottom line: even a universal service program as large as $70 billion a year could well produce social benefits in excess of that figure and thus represent a very real net economic and social gain for American society as a whole.

The gains from universal service would be realized only if the participants were doing valuable work.

Of course, the gains from universal service would be realized only if the participants were doing valuable work. And some fear that under a universal requirement, many participants in the civilian program in particular could be doing make-work (raking leaves is the image) without contributing much in the way of social value. Indeed, to the extent this happened—and some assert that it happens in the AmeriCorps program—the affected participants would come away from their service with a negative view of government and civic responsibility.

The concern is real. AmeriCorps tries to address it by decentralizing its activities, relying on both state governments and the private sector to develop programs that are essentially certified at the federal level. A civilian universal service program could work largely the same way, but on a much-expanded scale. At the same time, certain programs, especially those associated with homeland security, would have to be run out of Washington.

Still, it would be a challenge to develop meaningful work for all of the high school graduates who would enter the civilian program each year. Meeting this challenge provides another reason, besides cost, to begin the program on a less than universal scale, run it first as a lottery, and eventually expand it to a true universal system.

An Idea Whose Time Is Coming

Universal service is an idea whose time may not be quite here, but it is coming. For reasons of need, social cohesion, and social responsibility, universal service is a compelling idea. If adopted, it could be one of the truly transformative federal initiatives of recent times, perhaps having an even greater impact on American society than the GI bill, which helped educate much of the post–World War II generation. At the very least, universal service should be on the public agenda and actively debated. The discussion alone would be a fitting postscript to the horrible events of September 11 and the continuing search for ways to engage all Americans to serve their country.

A Bad Idea Whose Time Is Past

The Case Against Universal Service

BY BRUCE CHAPMAN
BROOKINGS REVIEW, FALL 2002

If each woman in China could only be persuaded to lower the hem of her skirt one inch, some 19th-century English merchants reasoned, the looms of Manchester could spin forever. Like that romantic calculation, the idea of universal service assumes a mythical economic and cultural system where people behave as you would like them to, with motivations of which you approve. Unlike it, universal service adds coercion to ensure compliance.

Universal service never was a good idea, and it grows worse with time. It fails militarily, morally, financially, and politically.

For almost a century, universal service has brought forth new advocates, each desiring to enlist all youth in something. Only the justifications keep changing. Today's justification is "homeland security." But is it realistic to suggest that youth who help guard a "public or private facility" (let alone those who stuff envelopes at some charity's office) are "shouldering the burden of war" in the same way as a soldier in Afghanistan?

I don't want to attach to Robert Litan all the customary arguments that universal service advocates have been promoting for years, especially because he states that "advocating universal service before September 11 would have been unthinkable" (at least to him). Except in times of mass conflict, such as the Civil War and the two World Wars, there has never been much of a reason for universal service. Still, the varied arguments for it need to be addressed.

No Military Case

Universal service is not needed on military grounds. We eliminated the draft three decades ago in part because the armed services found that they needed relatively fewer recruits to serve longer than conscription provided. As the numbers that were needed shrank, the unfairness of the draft became ever more apparent—and offensive. Youth, ever ingenious, found ways to get deferments, decamp to Canada, make themselves a nuisance to everyone in authority—and make those who did serve feel like chumps. Many of the young people who objected to military service availed themselves of alternative service, but no one seriously believed that most "conscientious objectors" were "shouldering the burden of war" in a way comparable to those fighting in the field.

> *Trying to justify universal service on moral grounds is . . . a mistake, and a serious one.*

The government took advantage of its free supply of almost unlimited manpower by underpaying its servicemen, thereby losing many recruits who might have chosen a military career. Raising the pay when the volunteer force was introduced changed the incentives and—surprise—eliminated the need for the draft. The all-volunteer force has been a big success.

Leaders in today's increasingly sophisticated, highly trained military now are talking of further manpower cuts. They have no interest in short-term soldiers of any kind and give no support to a return to conscription. The idea of using universal service to round up young men and women who, instead of direct military service, could be counted on to guard a "public or private facility," as Litan proposes, is naive. In Litan's plan, youth would be obligated for only a year—slightly less, if AmeriCorps were the model. Philip Gold, a colleague at Discovery Institute and author of the post–September 11 book *Against All Terrors: This Nation's Next Defense*, points out that "if the object is fighting, a person trained only for a few months is useless. In a noncombat defense position, he would be worse than useless. He would be dangerous."

Litan's interest in compulsory service grew partly out of recent work on Israel. According to Gold, armed guards in Israel do protect day care centers, for example. But all have had serious military training and two to three years of active duty, followed by service in the active reserves. A population with widespread military training and service can accomplish things that a civilian volunteer program cannot.

Litan anticipates nothing comparable from short-term universal servicemen and women. A one-year obligation, under the AmeriCorps example, works out to only 1,700 hours—roughly 10 months of 40-hour weeks. By the time the compulsory volunteers were trained, it would be time for them to muster out. The system would be roiled by constant turnover. It is surely unrealistic to expect to fill security jobs with youths who will be around for only a few months. Ask yourself, would you rather have a paid and trained person or a conscripted teenager inspecting the seaport for possible terrorists?

No Moral Justification

Trying to justify universal service on moral grounds is also a mistake, and a serious one. Morally, service isn't service to the extent it is compelled. Involuntary voluntarism is like hot snow. And allowing the pay to approach (let alone surpass) that available to ordinary workers of the same age performing the same tasks as the stipended and officially applauded "volunteers" stigmatizes the private sector. (The military recruit of today is sometimes called a volunteer only because he is not conscripted. His service is more commendable morally than that of some other paid employee because he is prepared to risk his life.)

Universal service advocates such as Litan are on especially shaky ground when charging that citizens should be "required to give something to their country in exchange for the full range of rights to which citizenship entitles them." This cuts against the grain of U.S. history and traditions. Citizens here are expected to be law-abiding, and they are called to jury duty—and to the military if absolutely necessary. They are encouraged (not forced) to vote and to render voluntary service—which Americans famously do. But to require such service before the rights of citizenship are extended is simply contrary to the purposes for which the country was founded and has endured. The Founders had a keen awareness of the ways that the state could tyrannize the people, and taking the people's liberty away to serve some specious government purpose unattached to national survival is a project that would horrify them.

I also raise this practical question: exactly which citizenship rights will Litan deny those people who decline to perform government-approved national service? What will be done to punish the activist who thinks he can do more to serve humanity through a political party than through prescribed government service? Or the young religious missionary who would rather save souls than guard a pier for a few months? How about—at the other end of the virtue spectrum—the young drug dealer who is only too happy to help guard the pier? Will you keep him out of the service of his choice and compel him to do rehab as his form of "service"?

Outside of mass mobilization for war—or in the special case of Israel, a small nation effectively on constant alert—the only modern nations that have conscripted labor to meet assorted, centrally decreed social purposes have been totalitarian regimes. In those lands, the object, as much as anything, has been to indoctrinate youth in the morality of the state. Litan may not have such goals in mind, but many universal service advocates want to use conscription to straighten out the next generation—to their approved standards. No doubt many—most?—think they can inculcate a sense of voluntary service through compulsory service.

In reality, however, no previous generation of youth has been so encouraged to volunteer for various approved, state-sponsored social causes. In many high schools in the United States, students cannot get a diploma without performing a certain number of hours of approved "community service." Does a child who must perform service to graduate from high school develop a high sense of what it means to help others? Does a student who learns that almost anything counts toward the service requirement—so long as he doesn't get paid—develop a keen sense of civil calling? Or does he hone his skill at gaming the system? And why, if we have this service requirement in high school—and some colleges—do we need yet another one for the year after high school?

Unintended Consequences

Universal service (indeed any national service scheme that achieves demographic heft) is a case study in unintended consequences. One surprise for liberals might be a growing disillusionment with the government and the way it wastes money. Today's youth trust the government and are immensely patriotic, but bureaucratized service requirements could cure that. Another unintended consequence might be instruction in how government makework is a tax on one's freedom and an irritating distraction from education goals and serious career development. Conservatives of a sardonic nature might come to appreciate the prospect of generations growing to adulthood with firsthand experience of government's impertinence. It would not be necessary thereafter to exhort the veterans of such unnecessary compulsion to resist the claims of government over the rest of their lives.

Universal service likewise would be an invitation to scandal. The military draft was bad enough, dispatching the budding scientist to pick up paper on a base's roadsides and sending the sickly malcontent to deliver meal trays to patients in base hospitals. People with powerful parents got cushy positions, while the poor got the onerous tasks. When labor is both free and abundant, it will be squandered and abused. If that was true in eras when mass armies were raised, what can one expect in a time when only a small fraction of the population is needed to operate our high-tech military?

No Financial Justification

The cost of universal service would be prohibitive. Direct costs would include those for assembling, sorting (and sorting out), allocating, and training several million youth in an unending manpower convoy. Indirect costs include clothing and providing initial medical attention, insurance, the law enforcement associated with such large numbers (no small expense in the army, even with presumably higher discipline), housing, and the periodic "leave" arrangements.

The $20,000 per involuntary volunteer estimated by Litan is too low. The more realistic total figure would be more like $27,000 to $30,000. First, the federal cost for a full-time AmeriCorps member is about $16,000, according to AmeriCorps officials. And that, recall, is for an average 10-month stint, so add another $3,000 or so for a 12-month term of service. (The $10,000 figure cited by Litan appears to average the cost of part-time volunteers with that of full-time volunteers.) Giving the involuntary volunteers the AmeriCorps education benefit of some $4,000 brings the total to about $23,000 of federal contribution for the full-time, one-year participant, which, with local or private match, will easily reach a total cost of some $30,000. Few unskilled young people just out of school make that in private employment!

Because organized compulsion costs more than real volunteering, however, the indirect expenses for governments would be still greater. Chief among these are the hidden financial costs of universal national service to the economy in the form of forgone labor. That problem plagued the old draft and would be more acute now. The United States has suffered a labor shortage for most of the past two decades, with the dearth of educated and trained labor especially serious. Yet universal service advocates want to pluck out of the employment ranks some 4 million people a year and apply a command-and-control approach to their optimal use. How can we even calculate the waste?

Litan says that in 1995 the GAO "positively evaluated" a cost-benefit study of three AmeriCorps programs that found them to produce quantifiable monetary benefits of $1.68 to $2.58 for every dollar invested. But Litan overstates the GAO's "positive evaluation" of the private study's findings. The GAO study merely analyzes the methodology of the private study based on the assumptions that are baked into it. These assumptions (of future benefits and their dollar values) are inherently "problematic," based as they are on "projected data." And neither the GAO nor the private study whose methodology it checked says anything about the applicability of the private study to some universal service program. Inferring GAO endorsement for some putative financial benefits from a national service scheme—let alone a program of compulsory national service—is not good economics.

By contrast, a recent review of the literature and evidence of government spending by William Niskanen, former chairman of the President's Council of Economic Advisors (under Ronald Reagan), concluded that "the marginal cost of government spending and taxes in the United States may be about $2.75 per additional dollar of tax revenue." As the late Nobel economist Frederick Hayek said, "There is only one problem with socialism. It does not work."

The cost of universal service for one year would not be $80 billion, with certain additional economic benefits, as Litan would have it, but roughly $120 billion, with considerable additional losses to the economy as a whole.

No Practical or Political Worth

There is no demand for all these volunteers, as charities themselves have pointed out. Nonprofits can absorb only so many unseasoned, unskilled, short-term "volunteers," particularly when some of the "volunteers" are reluctant, to say the least. So what is the point? Is it political?

Some universal service advocates (not Litan) have cited a January 2002 survey by Lake Snell Perry & Associates, The Tarrance Group, Inc. (The survey was conducted for the Center for Information and Research in Civic Learning & Engagement, the Center for Democracy & Citizenship, and The Partnership for Trust in Government at the Council for Excellence in Government.) The study shows strong support among youth for universal service. But these advocates usually neglect to mention that this support is based on a stated assumption in the survey question that such service would be "an alternative to (compulsory) military service should one be instituted." A truer reflection of youthful opinion is found in the survey's largely unreported question on community service as a requirement for high school graduation. That program is overwhelmingly opposed—by a 35 percent margin among current high school students. Interestingly, the same survey shows that "instituting civics and government course requirements in schools is favored by a 15-point margin by current high school students."

There is no demand for all these volunteers, as charities themselves have pointed out.

This should tell us something. Putting $120 billion, or even $80 billion, into a universal national service scheme would be a waste. But how about spending some tiny corner of that money on teaching kids about real—that is, voluntary—service? How about paying to teach students about representative democracy and their part in it as voters and volunteers or about the way our economy works and how to prepare for successful participation in it? Or to teach them American history (for many, it would be a new course) in a way that inspired them with the stories of men and women, great and humble, who have rendered notable service in their communities, nation, and world.

The way to get a nation of volunteers is to showcase voluntary service, praise it, reward it, and revere it. The way to sabotage voluntary service is to coerce it, bureaucratize it, nationalize it, cloak it in political correctness, and pay for it to the point where the "volunteer" makes out better than the poor soul of the same age who works for a living. Voluntary service blesses the one who serves as well as those to whom he renders service. Universal service would be civic virtue perverted into a civic vice.

Doing Disservice

BY DRAKE BENNETT
THE AMERICAN PROSPECT, OCTOBER 1, 2003

No matter what we do, those of us in our 20s can't seem to measure up to the Greatest Generation. That bygone nation of joiners, providers and world-beaters, in the standard story, puts to shame today's sad assemblage of narcissists and whiners. Gone are the days when the United States, stung by a Japanese sneak attack, rose up to shrug off the Great Depression and cohere into a fighting force of Riveting Rosies and Private Ryans. Political scientist Robert Putnam called our grandparents "the long civic generation."

Of course, the September 11 attacks did arouse a general sense of solidarity and national duty. According to the Progressive Policy Institute, there were, for example, three times as many volunteers for the national service program AmeriCorps as available slots. And despite the conventional wisdom that America's young are less civically engaged than their parents and grandparents, the reality is that young America is awash in community service. High-school and college community-service activities have never been more extensive. Many would build on this trend and dramatically expand existing service opportunities; some would even make a stint doing national service mandatory.

It's a venerable idea. For its supporters, national service does triple duty, shaping productive, selfless citizens and filling unmet social needs while creating a shared sense of national identity. As William James bracingly put it in a 1910 essay, "To coal and iron mines, to freight trains, to fishing fleets in December, to dishwashing, clothes-washing, and window-washing, to road-building and tunnel-making, to foundries and stoke-holes, and to frames of skyscrapers, would our gilded youths be drafted off, according to their choice, to get childishness knocked out of them, and to come back into society with healthier sympathies and soberer ideas."

President Bush himself has caught the national service bug. In his 2002 State of the Union address, he proposed expanding AmeriCorps by 50 percent, adding nearly $300 million to national service spending and creating spots for 2 million Americans in the country's national service programs by some unspecified date. Characteristically, there has been no follow-up. In fact, the House of Representatives voted down an emergency $100 million infusion

---

Reprinted with permission from Drake Bennett, "Doing Disservice," *The American Prospect*, Volume 14, Number 9: October 1, 2003. The American Prospect, 11 Beacon Street, Suite 1120, Boston, MA 02108. All rights reserved.

for cash-strapped AmeriCorps. As the memoirist-turned-service-advocate Dave Eggers wrote in a heartbroken *New York Times* op-ed, "Congress and the White House have turned their backs on these volunteers."

But the zeal of national service proponents is undimmed. The war on terrorism and its massive security needs, they argue, demand manpower of the sort that only a domestic army of community servants can supply. And the sense of threat has added urgency to discussions of national identity and solidarity, both issues that national service promises to address. The terrorist attacks only brought into relief a trend that has been accelerating for several years: In a growing number of states and school districts, community service is a requirement for high-school graduation, and "service learning" is the pedagogy of the day.

As a veteran of City Year—the community-service organization upon which then-President Bill Clinton based AmeriCorps—and one who counts my year of service a formative and productive one, I'm not sure that this epidemic of volunteerism is entirely a welcome trend. For starters, compulsory volunteering is a contradiction in terms. Also, systemic government solutions rather than piecemeal acts of goodwill better address many of the problems that volunteers tackle. If hospitals and libraries increasingly rely on volunteers, it's because reduced federal appropriations are starving institutions that depend on public funding. In this context, well-intentioned young people who fill the gap are enablers of the attack on public services.

Moreover, much of what's done by volunteers has a tacit politics that volunteerism may inadvertently conceal. If you volunteer in a soup kitchen or help the homeless, you should also be working to eliminate the causes of homelessness. That enterprise, of course, logically leads to social change and to politics as the necessary instrument of change. But many volunteer organizations, either because of their tax status, their funding sources or their necessary nonpartisanship, take great pains to eschew politics. A few years ago, when students affiliated with Phillips Brooks House, Harvard University's pre-eminent community-service institution for undergraduates, came out in support of the school's "living wage" campaign, they earned a rebuke from the university's new president, Lawrence Summers, for taking what he judged to be an overly partisan stand.

Local service projects—George Bush Senior's "thousand points of light"—fragment political energy. Yale Law School professors Bruce Ackerman and Anne Alstott, in their 1999 book, *The Stakeholder Society*, take contemporary liberals to task for their unwillingness to tackle the enormous and central problem of wealth inequality in favor of "a thousand lesser policies." Universal service seems to be a pretty good example of just that. Unlike conservatives, modern liberals are unafraid to use the government to take care of what the market can or will not. But to rely on an army of young amateurs to deal with societal needs seems a strangely indirect way to go about it. If inner-city schools are struggling, isn't the solution to give them more money for their infrastructures and teacher salaries instead of spending the money on an at best lightly trained conscript?

In addition, employers in both the public and private sectors, gifted with a national service corps of nearly 4 million, would be sorely tempted to use this pool of cheap, captive labor to phase out salaried (and benefited) employees. As Service Employees International Union lobbyist Skip Roberts dryly notes, "That might be the only reason why it might appeal to anyone in the White House."

But what of the character-building aspect of it? It's undeniable that some young people would have their first taste of service in such a program. However, with a vast majority of high schools participating in community service (83 percent, according to a 1999 study by the U.S. Department of Education), most students have already been exposed to the concept. And so far, research has failed to link even voluntary service with increased civic engagement. A recent study by the National Association of Secretaries of State found that youth who performed service were no more likely to be involved in politics than their nonvolunteering peers. The fact is, Americans between the ages of 15 and 25 already volunteer more than any other age group; but they also vote far less (and the number of voters continues to shrink). According to a 2002 study released by the University of Maryland's Center for Information & Research on Civic Learning & Engagement (CIRCLE), young Americans are also less likely than their (admittedly also pretty disengaged) elders to have participated in traditional forms of civic engagement—writing a letter to their congressman or newspaper, for example, or marching in a demonstration or volunteering for a political campaign.

Americans between the ages of 15 and 25 already volunteer more than any other age group; but they also vote far less.

When asked about this, the apolitical young respond that politics is, in effect, useless. Thomas Ehrlich is a former board member of the Corporation for National Service and a current scholar at the Carnegie Foundation for Teaching and Learning who studies civic engagement and service learning. He has found that "one of the reasons kids give [for their apolitical tendencies] is that they don't see a chance to make a difference. They can tutor a kid in school, clean up a park, serve in a community kitchen and feel that they're making a difference. But trying to change the political process in their community, much less the country—they don't see that happening."

Tellingly, the CIRCLE study found that the civic activities young people preferred were individual or non-governmental: buying a certain brand because they agreed with its values, for example, or donating to a charity. After all, as Michael Delli Carpini, a scholar of civic life and the dean of the University of Pennsylvania's Annenberg School for Communication, has noted, "Civic engagement has become *defined* as the one-on-one experience of working in a soup kitchen, clearing trash from a local river or tutoring a child once a week. What is missing is an awareness of the connection between the individual, isolated problems these actions are intended to address and the larger world of public policy." To enshrine what is in effect institutionalized volunteerism in a federal program could very well end up merely reinforcing the idea that acts of kindness, random or not, rather than governmental action, are the solution to society's ills.

And that is the central paradox of national service: It is big government for people who don't like big government—the counterpart of government support for local "faith-based" social services, or for traditional marriage as the cure for poverty. The current national service debate is really a holdover from the Clinton administration.

While liberals are rightly ambivalent about national service, it has gained supporters among self-styled "national greatness" conservatives, thinkers like William Kristol and David Brooks who are concerned with restoring America's sense of purpose and grandeur. For them, government is meant not so much to govern, or even to solve social ills, but to inspire and provide its citizens with a Teddy Roosevelt–like sense of resolve and destiny. Brooks, for example, has argued that what the federal government needs to focus on is building grand monuments and institutions like the Library of Congress.

Universal service would surely be an institution, and it would provide lots of people with a sense of purpose. But surely that's setting the bar pretty low for a federal program. As Tocqueville pointed out in the 1830s, America has always had a rich social fabric of voluntary institutions. The point of government is not to keep its citizens busy living lives of vigorous action but to do what markets cannot. Yet active government requires an activist public agenda, which in turn depends on activated voters. If there's a paucity of civic engagement among the young, it is less in the area of volunteering than in taking seriously the enterprise of citizenship.

A Nation of Servants

Defining Public Service for the Twenty-first Century

By Alan W. Dowd
WORLD & I, JANUARY 2004

There is a consensus in the United States that a key ingredient of maintaining a good society is involving Americans in service to something greater than themselves. The Founding Fathers believed it. Indeed, many of them sacrificed their lives—and, most of them, their wealth—for the greater cause of America's independence and nationhood. President John F. Kennedy awoke a generation with the phrase, "Ask not what your country can do for you; ask what you can do for your country." Some three decades later, President Bill Clinton declared, "Service is the spark to rekindle the spirit of democracy in an age of uncertainty." In the wake of the terrorist attacks on Washington and Manhattan, President George W. Bush challenged the American people to make "a commitment to service in [their] own communities. . . . Serve your country by tutoring or mentoring a child, comforting the afflicted, housing those in need of shelter and a home."[1]

Yet from the very beginning, the American people have valued the individual and rewarded individualism. After all, this is where the Pilgrims fled to find religious and political independence, the "Don't tread on me" flag once waved, homesteaders and frontiersmen daily redrew the borders of a nation, and the cowboy rode off into the sunset alone. Here free enterprise reigns and seemingly everyone is or once was an entrepreneur. As Alexis de Tocqueville concluded in *Democracy in America*, arguably the most insightful assessment of the American character ever written, "Individualism is a novel expression . . . a mature and calm feeling." The problem with individualism, according to de Tocqueville, is that it "saps the virtues of public life [and] in the long run . . . is absorbed in downright selfishness."[2]

What was true in the early nineteenth century remains true in the twenty-first. Unbridled individualism seems to have eaten away at that all-important connective tissue between employees and employers, shareholders and executives, neighbors and neighborhoods, citizens and government, old and young. Instead of shared values and common responsibilities, there is a demand for rights and entitlements, a selfish competition to acquire and amass, to consume and claim. Talk of public service is often dismissed as quaint. Indeed, as the National Commission on the Public Service concluded in January 2003, "The notion of public service, once a noble calling, proudly pursued by the most talented Americans of every generation, draws an indifferent response from today's young people and repels many of the country's leading private citizens."[3]

> *Public service is both more and less than working for some government agency or winning an election.*

However, there remains a pull in the other direction, an undercurrent of cooperation and community that often redirects America's individualist impulse. This ebb and flow has always existed and was grafted into the very marrow of the United States: Although America's founding document was a declaration of independence, arguing that each person has a right to life, liberty, and the pursuit of his own happiness, the U.S. Constitution begins with the phrase "We the people," not "I the individual."

The challenge today, as in Jefferson and Madison's day, as in Kennedy's, is to strike a balance between these two competing forces—and to do so without expanding the size and scope of government any further. A first step in that direction is to recognize that anyone can participate in public service.

From Bill Buckley to Bill Clinton

It may be helpful to define what public service is before considering how it contributes to a good society. Public service is both more and less than working for some government agency or winning an election. That's because serving the public demands more than simply taking an oath or wearing a uniform. Paradoxically, authentic public service doesn't require a citizen to enlist in the military, run for office, or join the Peace Corps. For that matter, it doesn't require a person to be a citizen: There are 31,000 foreign nationals serving in the U.S. armed forces. In fact, as the *Wall Street Journal* reported last spring, some of the very first American troops to die in Iraq weren't Americans at all, but rather immigrants such as Marine Corporal José Antonio Gutierrez from Guatemala.[4]

Some expressions of public service are obvious: elective or judicial office, military service, national service programs. Some are not so obvious. The schoolteacher, Social Security official, police officer or deputy sheriff, precinct committeeman, librarian, and juror are all public servants, whether we notice them or not.

So what is a good definition for public service? A dictionary entry points us in the right direction: Public service is simply "a service rendered in the public interest." By that definition, virtually anyone can be a public servant—no matter what his station in life.

If an action promotes the public good or meets the public's needs, it is public service. If it promotes something else or meets only private needs, it is something less than public service—no matter who is performing it.

This expansive definition calls to mind Justice Potter Stewart's wry observation on obscenity: "I know it when I see it." In the same way, public service may not be easily defined, but we know it when we see it.

> *Perhaps our concept of public service—focused as it is on government and politics—is too narrow.*

Simply put, perhaps our concept of public service—focused as it is on government and politics—is too narrow. Consider the heroes of Flight 93, who died so that hundreds or thousands of other Americans might live. They weren't soldiers or statesmen, but they certainly served the public. Just as September 11 taught us that war is no longer something fought "over there," it should have reminded us that public service is not something performed exclusively by public officials, people in uniform, or politicians. It's something that every American can—and arguably should—do, which may explain Washington's numerous attempts to create and enlarge national-service programs.

Today, there are bills working their way through Congress that would create a National Youth Service Day, modernize the Peace Corps, revamp and streamline the well-known AmeriCorps program, reorganize all federal service programs, form a civilian-service corps styled after "the best aspects of military service,"[5] and enlarge AmeriCorps. As the Corporation for National and Community Service details in its "History of National Service," this is nothing new: In 1910, U.S. philosopher William James called for the "conscription of the whole youthful population to form for a certain number of years a part of the army enlisted against nature." Twenty-three years later, FDR's Civilian Conservation Corps did just that.

What the post-FDR government service programs lacked in utopian rationale, they made up for in sheer numbers. Kennedy created the Peace Corps in 1961 to deploy young Americans around the world on humanitarian missions. Not to be outdone, President Lyndon Johnson established VISTA, the National Teacher Corps, JobCorps, and other military-sounding organizations to wage his war on poverty. The Youth Conservation Corps was formed in 1970, followed by the Young Adult Conservation Corps in 1978. In the 1980s, Campus Outreach Opportunity League, Youth Service America, and other organizations were founded at the local level to attract young people to service. By 1990, President George H.W. Bush had launched the federal Points of Light Foundation and opened the Office of National Service inside the White House. Clinton commissioned the first 20,000 AmeriCorps workers in 1994. By the time he left office, some 200,000 Americans had participated in the program—at a cost to taxpayers of about $15,000 each.

Yet after seventy years of federal service programs, proponents of national service still complain that not enough Americans are serving and those who do aren't serving enough. Their solution is not to pause and reconsider the slide toward mandated service but to propose newer, larger programs that expand Washington's role in our lives.

Indeed, it seems that a narrow definition of public service often leads to the expansion of government, while an expansive definition of public service helps to limit the size of government and bring about the balance described at the outset of this essay. Think about it: If public service is something that only people connected to government or politics can do, then the only way to ensure that Americans are serving is for them to contribute more time to the state or for the state to create more opportunities for public service.

Consider, as evidence, the embattled AmeriCorps program. Whatever your opinion of AmeriCorps, it is difficult to deny that the program is premised on the notion that government is the critical link between the individual and his capacity to serve. Last summer, for example, some two hundred corporate leaders published an open letter to the president and Congress lauding the record of AmeriCorps and warning that its ranks would shrink by thousands in 2004 if the federal government didn't fork over $200 million in new spending. Without the government's help, the CEOs seemed to argue, Americans can't—or won't—serve their fellow citizens.

The CEOs are not alone in viewing service through the prism of government. In the post–September 11 milieu, Bush created USAFreedomCorps to serve as an umbrella for all national service programs. "As a Coordinating Council housed at the White House and chaired by President George W. Bush," the USAFreedomCorps Web site explains, "we are working to strengthen our culture of service and help find opportunities for every American to start volunteering."

In 2001, Sens. Evan Bayh and John McCain coauthored the first Call to Service Act, which would have ballooned the AmeriCorps program more than fivefold—from 40,000 workers in 2001 to 250,000 in 2010. (That bill did not become law, but a newer version of it is now in Congress.) "Americans again are eager for ways to serve at home and abroad," the senators explained. "Government should make it easier for them to do so."[6] In other words, before we can help others, Washington needs to help us.

In 1998, President Bill Clinton concluded that AmeriCorps "has given 100,000 young people the opportunity to serve their country"—as if no such opportunity existed before the creation of the program.[7]

Almost a decade earlier, William Buckley wrote a lengthy defense of what might be called "nearly mandatory" national service in his book *Gratitude*. He based his argument on the premise that "everyone who receives the protection of society owes a return for the benefit."[8] Buckley was quick to reject "compulsory national service." He argued instead that government could use sanctions and inducements to promote national service without mandating it. For example, Buckley noted that the federal government could withhold financial aid and state governments could withhold or revoke driver's licenses from those who were unwilling to serve, while tax breaks could be offered to those who join up.[9]

Of course, these sanctions and inducements, it seems, would have the effect of making such service mandatory. What 18-year-old would rather surrender his driver's license than enlist in the "National Service Corps"? What college student would choose to cough up $10,000 in loans or cash if he could save it by joining a nearly mandatory government-service program?

The idea of mandated service certainly has currency. Already, some high schools and colleges require students to perform school-approved "volunteer work" prior to graduating. Some employers are mandating the same of employees. When they promoted their supersized AmeriCorps in 2001–2002, Bayh and McCain argued that "national service should one day be a rite of passage for young Americans."[10]

Given all the blessings and opportunities afforded us as Americans, one can hardly argue with the goals of Bush, Bayh, McCain, Buckley, and other proponents of national service. We do owe our country "a return for the benefit." Nor can their motives be called into question. As the grandson of a senator and son of a president, Bush has public service flowing through his veins. McCain, whose father and grandfather were naval officers, flew combat missions in Vietnam and was a POW prior to serving in Washington. The son of a senator, Bayh has been in government service most of his adult life. Buckley was an Army draftee at the end of World War II, a candidate for elective office, and a presidential emissary, but he arguably has done more for his country outside of government, as a writer and thinker—which underscores the broader point here: One doesn't have to serve the government to serve his country. Moreover, short of an imminent threat to the nation, a citizen should not be compelled to serve his country by anything more than his conscience. If he is, his actions won't have much meaning. As the Roman philosopher Seneca wrote, "To repay gratitude is a most praiseworthy act." However, "it ceases to be praiseworthy if it is made obligatory."[11]

> *Short of an imminent threat to the nation, a citizen should not be compelled to serve his country by anything more than his conscience.*

For those Americans who believe government is the glue that holds everything else in place, national service is a solution to the problem of apathy. But for those Americans who believe the individual has rights to exercise free from government interference, and responsibilities to fulfill free from government coercion, mandated national service is a solution in search of a problem.

The Mission Matters

This brings us to the matter of military conscription, a popular solution to the supposed public-service deficit, especially among those who advocate some type of mandated service yet are critical of bloated AmeriCorps-style programs. Citing everything from the need for a common civic experience and the decline of patriotism to racial inequality and the dearth of military acumen among members of Congress (in 1971, veterans accounted for 71 percent of Congress; today, it's less than 34 percent), a growing and eclectic group is advocating a return to the draft. Unfortunately, it is trying to bring back the draft for all the wrong reasons.

Keeping a promise he made in his 1968 presidential campaign, President Richard Nixon ended the draft in December 1972. Aside for a brief interregnum after World War II and before the Korean War, it had been in effect for the previous three decades. It was expensive, unpopular, and, counterintuitively, unfair. "Military draftees and recruits lost millions of man-years in places like Kiska, Alaska, belowdecks on some stinking supply ship in the Pacific, or stenciling jeeps at Fort Ord in California," recalls historian Derek Leebaert in *The Fifty-Year Wound*. As a consequence, Leebaert concludes, "Most of these men's first impression of public service was that it wasted their time. Later, when others were conscripted after them, they believed it wasted their money as well." Moreover, thanks to its many loopholes and exemptions, the draft gave Vietnam the dubious distinction of being the first (and hopefully last) major conflict in U.S. history in which the wealthiest Americans were not proportionately represented on the battlefield.[12]

To fix these problems, the Pentagon replaced the draft with an all-volunteer force (AVF). The thinking was that a military composed solely of people who wanted to serve—even if it was smaller—would be more effective and efficient at performing its mission than one made up of people who would rather be somewhere else. This was an untested theory, but it proved to be sound.

Thirty years later, the U.S. military is more lethal, more flexible, more motivated, leaner, and smarter than it has ever been. In fact, according to a recent Pentagon briefing, "Virtually all officers have to be college graduates; a high fraction of our officers actually have master's degrees and a small fraction have Ph.D.s."[13] Moreover, every soldier, sailor, airman, and Marine wants to serve. As Fred Peck, a military writer and retired Marine, wryly observes, "In today's AVF . . . it's a punishment to kick people out. In the draft era it was a punishment to keep them in."[14] Most important of all, the AVF is without peer on the global battlefield.

That is, after all, the mission of the U.S. military—to deter and, if necessary, destroy America's enemies on the field of battle. It is not to restore America's civic spirit, serve as a training ground for congressmen, or give young people a sense of purpose and a taste of patriotism. If the military achieves the latter as a by-product of the former—as in the 1940s—then so much the better. However, when we try to use the military to achieve some nonmilitary social aim—no matter how honorable—we often do more harm than good, as America learned during the ferocious and unnecessary fights over gays in the military and women in combat.

Consider Rep. Charles Rangel's quixotic effort in 2003 to reinstate the draft. By his own admission, he wasn't motivated by a desire to make sure the Pentagon had the manpower to meet the rising demands of war. In fact, Rangel was an opponent of the war in Iraq and is a critic of much of the rest of the Bush administration's antiterror campaign. Instead of helping the Pentagon, Rangel wanted to make sure Americans "shoulder the burden of war equally," which sounds reasonable. Who could argue with the principle of shared sacrifice? According to Rangel, himself a combat veteran, "A disproportionate number of the poor and members of minority groups make up the enlisted ranks of the military," and hence bear a heavier burden in times of war. Renewing the draft, he concluded last spring, would spread that burden across U.S. society and force the nation's leaders to be more cautious.[15]

Rangel was operating under a false premise, however. As Mackubin Owens, a professor at the Naval War College, explains, "The claim of disproportionate minority casualties wasn't true during the Vietnam War . . . [and] it is even less true today." In Vietnam, 86 percent of the Americans killed were white; 12.5 percent were black, which was actually less than the corresponding census numbers of 13.1 percent.[16] In today's wars, where pilots and Special Forces do much of the fighting and dying, the numbers are even less reflective of the country as a whole—but not in the manner Rangel would have us believe: As a *USA Today* analysis revealed, African-Americans comprise about 2 percent of Air Force pilots, 2.5 percent of Navy pilots, 5 percent of Army Green Berets, and 10.6 percent of Army combat infantrymen.[17]

Given the global war on terror, stabilization missions in Iraq and Afghanistan, looming challenges on the Korean Peninsula, and decades-old commitments in Europe and the Pacific, a revived military draft may yet be necessary. But that decision should be based on military needs, not political misconceptions or desirable social aims.

Rangel has every right to oppose this war and the next, although it's regrettable that he chose to use race to make his case. After all, splitting America and its military into a racial kaleidoscope doesn't promote much unity. And without unity, it's hard to promote service to a cause greater than self—and even harder to win a war.

Now and Then

Indeed, proponents of government-centered service programs are quick to argue that Americans are too self-centered to think about others, too oblivious and distracted to care about their country, too soft to sacrifice, that we lack the inclination to serve which characterized earlier generations. At first glance, they appear to be right: During World War II, my grandfathers and their generation marched off to Africa, Europe, and the Pacific's mosaic of islands and reefs. Some 400,000 of them never returned. On the home front, the wives, sweethearts, and sisters of America's fighting men served their country by donating metal and tin, giving up their nylon stockings, making do with bald tires and meatless Mondays, rationing gasoline, and forming an army of their own to operate the country's armament factories.

In the war on terror, by contrast, Uncle Sam hasn't made any such demands of the American people. In fact, during those first months after the attacks on Manhattan and the Pentagon, as the economy staggered, Bush urged Americans to "visit Disney World and America's other vacation spots." Congress passed an array of wartime tax cuts to prime the pump of American consumerism. Automakers, hotels, and airlines offered enticing packages to pry open our wallets and "keep America moving." What's more, there's no military draft; there's not even a push to recruit more troops. Service to country seems like little more than a punch line.

Nevertheless, post–September 11 America is not all that different from post–Pearl Harbor America. Consider a collection of World War II–era polling data unearthed by *American Enterprise* magazine. In 1942, after a year of fighting, only 23 percent of Americans said they had volunteered for civilian defense programs. In 1944, 66 percent of Americans said their fellow citizens weren't taking the war seriously enough, and 45 percent said they went about their business as if there were no war at all. In 1945, fully 64 percent of Americans said they had not made any real sacrifice for the war.[18] Leebaert adds, "After two years of fighting, nearly a third of the country did not know that the Philippines had fallen, and twice that many had never hear of the Atlantic Charter."[19]

Free and Good

The purpose here is not to smear the "golden age" of service, sacrifice, and civic patriotism but rather to put things in perspective. Americans are individualistic and somewhat distrustful of government by nature. Hence, they don't flock to government-service programs. When government stays out of the way, however, they do serve and sacrifice for each other. As de Tocqueville observed, it is freedom itself that "leads a great number of citizens to value the affection of their neighbors and their kindred, perpetually brings men together, and forces them to help one another in spite of the propensities that sever them."[20]

According to the eminent nonprofit scholar Richard Cornuelle, Americans have always wanted a nation that is both free and good. Writing in his landmark work *Reclaiming the American Dream*, he notes that "our founders took pains to design a government with limited power, and then carefully scattered the forces which could control it." That would help nurture freedom. To promote a good society, "We developed a genius for solving common problems. People joined together in bewildering combinations to found schools, churches, opera houses, co-ops, hospitals, to build bridges and canals, to help the poor."[21]

> *"The service motive is at least as powerful as the desire for profit or power."*—Richard Cornuelle, nonprofit scholar

Our ancestors were committed to living independent lives, but to survive and thrive they also had to be interdependent. The result was, in a sense, a nation of servants.

According to Cornuelle, "The service motive is at least as powerful as the desire for profit or power."[22] Like the profit motive, it can be curbed or encouraged by external forces: Just as burdensome tax policies, corruption, and regulations can stifle an individual's desire to make a profit, the government's co-opting of public service can stifle an individual's desire to serve. In other words, if government does too much, it could have the effect of discouraging people from serving their neighbor and nation. It is basic human nature that when a neighbor's needs appear to be met, the desire to serve ebbs. People simply won't take an active part in their nation or their neighborhoods if someone or something else is already playing that role. If, as de Tocqueville argued, "personal interest is restrained when confronted by the sight of other men's misery," then the converse is true as well: Personal interest is unleashed when that misery or need is being met by something else, especially the state. Once unleashed, it grows into the selfishness that de Tocqueville feared and today's advocates of government-endorsed, taxpayer-financed national service are right to criticize.[23]

Americans have combated this selfishness not with government but with a vast array of what de Tocqueville called associations and free institutions—nongovernment organizations that keep us connected to each other and keep the government at bay. These organizations remind us "that it is the duty as well as the interest of men to make themselves useful to their fellow creatures."[24] This is the essence of public service—to be useful to your fellowman—and despite the smothering embrace of government, Americans continue to fulfill this duty.

According to studies conducted by the Independent Sector, a coalition of nonprofit groups, there are 1.6 million charities, social welfare organizations, and religious congregations in the United States. The number of American adults who volunteer in any given year ranges between 84 million and 110 million. Together, this army of volunteers works 15.5 billion man-hours a year, representing the equivalent of over 9 million full-time employees. Astonishingly, they aren't being induced or paid to serve; they are able to serve without any guidance from Washington; and they are more effective and far less expensive than their counterparts in government-run programs.[25]

The evidence is all around us. Consider the Habitat for Humanity branch that builds homes for the homeless and hopeless, the church that delivers food to shut-ins, the law firm that does pro bono work for immigrants and paupers, the physicians group that quietly pro-

> ## *The line between public service and the private sector ... is rapidly blurring.*

vides "charity care," the clinic that donates supplies to a school nurse's office, the foundation that helps build universities and hospitals, the business that partners with a community group to clean up a neighborhood, the Little League dads and Scout moms who teach values of good citizenship and hard word to the children in their care, or, for that matter, any parent. As the British progressive George Bernard Shaw concluded, "Perhaps the greatest social service that can be rendered by anybody to this country and to mankind is to bring up a family."

All of these people and institutions serve the public in some significant way, and this is just the tip of the iceberg. The line between public service and the private sector—indeed, between government and nongovernment service—is rapidly blurring, as faith-based organizations and corporations partner with federal, state, and local governments to provide goods and services that once were the sole responsibility of government.

For example, according to *Government Executive* magazine, the Pentagon is increasingly "hiring contractors to provide support behind the lines." Companies such as Brown and Root are based alongside U.S. forces throughout the Balkans. They repair vehicles, build barracks, operate convenience stores, manage 95 percent of the Army's rail lines and airfields, cook meals, wash laundry, and, in the words of one employee, "do everything that does not require us to carry a gun." *Government Executive* found that for every two troops deployed in the Balkans, there are three contractors. A little over a decade ago, by way of comparison, there was just one contractor for every one hundred troops in the Gulf.[26] Today, there is one contractor for every ten troops in Iraq.[27] Everywhere they are deployed, both the troops and the contractors are in harm's way, as a flurry of prewar attacks underscored last January. A civilian contractor based at Camp Doha in Kuwait was killed, another wounded, during the buildup.

The employees of these quasi-government organizations and government subcontractors are in a sense public servants. They may be public servants twice removed, but they're still serving the public.

Balance

Every American has the capacity and opportunity to serve something greater than self, and countless millions do so everyday. Sometimes they do so through government, but often they do not. If the goal is to maintain a good society, or to build a better society, then counteracting selfishness with service is indeed important. However, Washington does not need to pass new legislation, restart the draft, or create new programs to achieve that balance. In fact, rather than expanding programs, Washington needs to expand its definition of public service. As the poet Robert Browning observed, "All service ranks the same with God."

Endnotes

1. George W. Bush, Nov. 8, 2001, www.whitehouse.gov.
2. Alexis de Tocqueville, *Democracy in America* (New York: Modern Library, 1981), 395.
3. National Commission on the Public Service, final report *Urgent Business for America; Revitalizing the Federal Government for the 21st Century*, available online at www.maxwell.syr.edu/gpp/grade/2002fall.asp.
4. See "Immigrant Soldiers," *Wall Street Journal*, April 4, 2003; Brendan Mintier, "Jose Antonio Gutierrez," *Wall Street Journal*, April 4, 2003.
5. See S.1274, the Call to Service Act of 2003.
6. Evan Bayh and John McCain, "A New Start for National Service," *New York Times*, Nov. 6, 2001.
7. Bill Clinton, "Nurturing Citizens Service," U.S. Society and Values, *USIA Electronic Journal*, Sept. 1998.
8. William F. Buckley, *Gratitude* (New York: Random House, 1990), 18.
9. Buckley, *Gratitude*, 141–45.
10. Bayh and McCain, "A New Start."
11. Seneca, "On Benefits," in: *Moral Essays*, trans. J.W. Basore (Cambridge: Harvard University Press, 1989), 137.
12. Derek Leebaert, *The Fifty-Year Wound*, (Boston: Little Brown & Co., 2002), xii, 357.
13. Pentagon briefing on the All-Volunteer Force, Jan. 13, 2003, www.defenselink.mil.

14. Fred Peck, "The Draft Debate," *American Legion Magazine*, June 2003.
15. Charles Rangel, "Bring Back the Draft," *New York Times*, Dec. 31, 2002.
16. Mackubin Owens, "The Color of Combat," *National Review* Online, Oct. 4, 2003.
17. Tom Squitieri and Dave Moniz, "Front-line Troops Disproportionately White, not Black; Numbers Refute Long-held Belief," *USA Today*, Jan. 21, 2003.
18. "Opinion Pulse," *American Enterprise*, Jan./Feb. 2003, 62.
19. Leebaert, *The Fifty-Year Wound*, 7.
20. De Tocqueville, *Democracy in America*, 401.
21. Richard Cornuelle, *Reclaiming the American Dream* (New Brunswick: Transaction Publishers, 1965), 21.
22. Cornuelle, *Reclaiming the American Dream*, 61.
23. De Tocqueville, *Memoir on Pauperism* (Chicago: Ivan Dee Publishers, 1997), 56.
24. De Tocqueville, *Democracy in America*, 402.
25. Independent Sector, "Giving and Volunteering in the United States in 2001," independentsector.org; "The New Nonprofit Almanac in Brief: Facts and Figures on the Independent Sector 2001," independentsector.org.
26. George Cahlink, "Army of Contractors," *Government Executive*, Feb. 1, 2002.
27. Kenneth Bredemeier, "Thousands of Private Contractors Support U.S. Forces in Persian Gulf," *Washington Post*, March 3, 2003.

Appendix

Statement Upon Signing Order Establishing the Peace Corps

(Executive Order 10924)

PRESIDENT JOHN F. KENNEDY
MARCH 1, 1961

I have today signed an Executive Order providing for the establishment of a Peace Corps on a temporary pilot basis. I am also sending to Congress a message proposing authorization of a permanent Peace Corps. This Corps will be a pool of trained American men and women sent overseas by the U.S. Government or through private institutions and organizations to help foreign countries meet their urgent needs for skilled manpower.

It is our hope to have 500 or more people in the field by the end of the year.

The initial reactions to the Peace Corps proposal are convincing proof that we have, in this country, an immense reservoir of such men and women—anxious to sacrifice their energies and time and toil to the cause of world peace and human progress.

In establishing our Peace Corps we intend to make full use of the resources and talents of private institutions and groups. Universities, voluntary agencies, labor unions and industry will be asked to share in this effort—contributing diverse sources of energy and imagination—making it clear that the responsibility for peace is the responsibility of our entire society.

We will only send abroad Americans who are wanted by the host country—who have a real job to do—and who are qualified to do that job. Programs will be developed with care, and after full negotiation, in order to make sure that the Peace Corps is wanted and will contribute to the welfare of other people. Our Peace Corps is not designed as an instrument of diplomacy or propaganda or ideological conflict. It is designed to permit our people to exercise more fully their responsibilities in the great common cause of world development.

Life in the Peace Corps will not be easy. There will be no salary and allowances will be at a level sufficient only to maintain health and meet basic needs. Men and women will be expected to work and live alongside the nationals of the country in which they are stationed—doing the same work, eating the same food, talking the same language.

But if the life will not be easy, it will be rich and satisfying. For every young American who participates in the Peace Corps—who works in a foreign land—will know that he or she is sharing in the great common task of bringing to man that decent way of life which is the foundation of freedom and a condition of peace.

NOTE: The President departed substantially from this written text in his spoken remarks.

National Service Timeline

Read about the history of national service—from the creation of the Civilian Conservation Corps in 1933 to the launch of the President's Volunteer Service Award in 2003. This timeline provides a quick glance at key dates and milestones during the past century.

1903: The Cooperative Education Movement is founded at the University of Cincinnati.

Circa 1905: American philosophers William James and John Dewey develop intellectual foundations for service-based learning.

1910: American philosopher William James envisions non-military national service in his essay "The Moral Equivalent of War."

1933–1942: Franklin D. Roosevelt creates the Civilian Conservation Corps (CCC), providing opportunities for millions of young men to serve six to 18 months to help restore the nation's parks, revitalize the economy, and support their families and themselves.

1935: The Works Progress Administration, later renamed the Work Projects Administration, is established to provide work-relief for millions of unemployed Americans.

1944: The GI Bill, officially known as the Servicemen's Readjustment Act of 1944, is created, linking service and education and offering Americans educational opportunity in return for service to their country.

1960s: Demonstration projects for the Retired and Senior Volunteer Program (RSVP), the Foster Grandparent Program, and the Senior Companion Program (which together are known today as Senior Corps) are launched to demonstrate the effectiveness of the service model and to engage older Americans in a range of service activities.

1961: President John F. Kennedy proposes establishment of the Peace Corps and Congress authorizes it on September 22, 1961. President Kennedy states, "The wisdom of this idea is that someday we'll bring it home to America."

The White House Conference on Aging is held, drawing attention to the continuing opportunity and need to engage older adults in meaningful service activities.

1964: As part of the "War on Poverty," President Lyndon B. Johnson creates VISTA (Volunteers in Service to America), a National Teacher Corps, the Job Corps, and University Year of Action.

1965: College work-study programs are established to harness the energy and enthusiasm of young people in communities.

Source: Web site of the Corporation for National & Community Service (*www.nationalservice.org*)

The Older Americans Act of 1965 is passed (an outcome of the 1961 White House Conference on Aging). The Act sparked interest in creating programs for older adults and insuring their continued contribution to society.

The Foster Grandparent Program begins as a national demonstration effort to show how low-income persons aged 60 and over can establish meaningful relationships with children in need.

The Community Service Society of New York launches a pilot project involving a group of older adults in volunteer service to their communities. The project demonstrates the value of senior volunteers and serves as a precursor to the Retired Senior Volunteer Program.

1966: Urban Corps emerges, funded with federal work-study dollars.

By this time, 3,600 VISTA members are serving throughout the country, helping to develop the first Head Start programs and Job Corps sites, and starting agricultural cooperatives, community groups, and small businesses.

1966–1967: The phrase "service-learning" is first used to describe a project in East Tennessee that links students and faculty with area development organizations.

1968: The National Service Secretariat Conference on National Service is held in Washington, D.C.

Foster Grandparent projects grow to 40 states and Puerto Rico, enrolling 4,100 Foster Grandparents and assisting more than 10,000 children in health, education, welfare, and related settings.

1969: Retired Senior Volunteer Program was authorized under Title VI of the Older Americans Act.

1968–1971: Two Senior Companion demonstration projects, funded by the U.S. Department of Health, Education and Welfare, and the Administration on Aging, are launched in Tampa, Florida, and Cincinnati, Ohio.

1970s: In 1970, the Youth Conservation Corps engages 38,000 people ages 14 to 18 in summer environmental programs.

VISTA merges with the Peace Corps and senior service programs to form the ACTION agency.

1971: The White House Conference on Youth Report calls for linking service and learning. The National Center for Public Service Internships, the Society for Field Experience Education, and the National Student Volunteer Program are established.

The Retired Senior Volunteer Program (RSVP) is launched in the spring and 11 projects begin by summer.

1972: More than 10,000 Foster Grandparents are enrolled in 133 projects in all 50 states, the District of Columbia, Puerto Rico, and the Virgin Islands.

1973: The Foster Grandparent Program, the Retired Senior Volunteer Program, and the Senior Companion Program are authorized under the Domestic Volunteer Service Act of 1973.

The Retired Senior Volunteer Program grows to 590 projects nationwide.

1974: The Retired Senior Volunteer Program grows to 666 projects nationwide.

Eighteen model Senior Companion projects are funded.

1975: More than 1,000 Senior Companions are serving in projects. More than 60 percent serve in private homes.

1976: California Governor Jerry Brown establishes the California Conservation Corps, the first non-federal youth corps at the state level.

1977–1978: Existing Senior Companions projects are expanded, and 28 new projects are funded, creating opportunities for 3,000 Senior Companions to assist 9,500 clients in 39 states. In-home assignments grow to 65 percent.

1978: The Young Adult Conservation Corps creates small conservation corps in the states with 22,500 participants age 16 to 23.

1979: National Student Volunteer Program becomes the National Center for Service-Learning.

1980s: National service efforts are launched at the grassroots level, including the Campus Outreach Opportunity League (1984) and Campus Compact (1985), which help mobilize students in higher education; the National Association of Service and Conservation Corps (1985), which helps replicate youth corps in states and cities; and Youth Service America (1985), through which many young people are provided the opportunity to serve.

VISTA's focus changes to encourage citizen participation and community self-help.

1980–1987: Forty-two new Senior Companion projects are funded, and approximately 81 percent of placements are in-home assignments.

1981: National Center for Service-Learning for Early Adolescents is established.

1986: The VISTA Literacy Corps is developed to create literacy councils and expand adult education.

1988: The Retired Senior Volunteer Program grows to 750 projects nationwide, with approximately 400,000 senior volunteers participating.

The Senior Companion Program grows to 173 projects nationwide, with more than 8,000 senior volunteers participating.

1989–1990: President George H. W. Bush creates the Office of National Service in the White House and the Points of Light Foundation to foster volunteering.

1990: President Bush signs the National and Community Service Act of 1990 into law. The legislation authorizes grants to schools to support service-learning through Serve America (now known as Learn and Serve America) and demonstration grants for national service programs to youth corps, nonprofits, and colleges and universities.

1992: A bipartisan group of Senators drafts legislation to create the National Civilian Community Corps as a way to explore how to use post–Cold War military resources to help solve problems here at home.

The Maryland State Board of Education adopts a mandatory service requirement to graduate from high school.

1993: The Association of Supervision and Curriculum Development endorses the importance of linking service with learning.

September 1993: President Bill Clinton signs the National and Community Service Trust Act of 1993, creating AmeriCorps and the Corporation for National and Community Service to expand opportunities for Americans to serve their communities. VISTA and the National Civilian Community Corps become part of AmeriCorps, and the Foster Grandparent Program, the Retired and Senior Volunteer Program, and the Senior Companion Program are combined to create Senior Corps.

With passage of National and Community Service Act, Congress changes Retired Senior Volunteer Program to Retired "and" Senior Volunteer program to reflect that not all volunteers were retired.

Governor-appointed state service commissions are created to administer AmeriCorps funding at the state level.

1994: The Corporation for National and Community Service officially begins operation.

Congress passes the King Holiday and Service Act of 1994, charging the Corporation for National and Community Service with establishing Martin Luther King Day as a day of service.

The Stanford Service-Learning Institute is created.

The Ford Foundation/United Negro College Fund Community Service Partnership Project (a 10-college program linking direct service and learning) begins.

Four National Civilian Community Corps campuses open in Aberdeen, MD; Charleston, SC; Denver, CO; and San Diego, CA.

September 1994: The first class of AmeriCorps members—20,000 strong—begins serving in more than 1,000 communities. In swearing in these Americans, President Clinton says: "Service is a spark to rekindle the spirit of democracy in an age of uncertainty. When it is all said and done, it comes down to three simple questions: What is right? What is wrong? And what are we going to do about it? Today you are doing what is right—turning your words into deeds."

1995: A study commissioned by the IBM Foundation, the Charles A. Dana Foundation, and the James Irvine Foundation finds that every federal dollar invested in AmeriCorps results in $1.60 to $2.60 or more in direct, measurable benefits to AmeriCorps members and the communities they serve.

The Service-Learning network is established on the Internet, via the University of Colorado Peace Studies Center.

The National Civilian Community Corps is included under AmeriCorps, becoming AmeriCorps*NCCC. The Aberdeen, MD, campus moves to Perry Point, MD.

April 1997: The Presidents' Summit for America's Future, chaired by General Colin Powell, brings together President Clinton, former Presidents Bush, Ford, and Carter, and Mrs. Reagan to encourage increased service and volunteerism to meet the needs of America's youth.

1997: AmeriCorps expands by introducing the Education Awards Program, which allows more organizations to join the service network—nonprofits, faith-based organizations, colleges and universities, welfare-to-work programs, and other groups.

The Fourth of July Declaration on the Civic Responsibility of Higher Education and the Wingspread Declaration Renewing the Civic Mission of the American University are published.

President Clinton and former President George Bush announce the resumption of the Daily Points of Light Award.

A fifth AmeriCorps*NCCC campus opens in Washington, D.C.

American Association of State Service Commissions (ASC) was launched.

1999: Since the program began, more than 100,000 AmeriCorps members have served 33 million people in 4,000 communities.

October 1999: AmeriCorps celebrates five years and 150,000 members. General Colin Powell, Utah's Governor Mike Leavitt, Coretta Scott King, and Sargent Shriver join President Clinton at the White House to honor the winners of the first All*AmeriCorps awards.

June 2000: The Foster Grandparent Program commemorates its 35th anniversary. As the Senior Companion Program enters its 26th year of service, and RSVP looks ahead to its 30th birthday in 2001, the three National Senior Service Corps programs engage more than 500,000 adults age 55 and older in sharing their time and talents to help meet local community needs.

October 2000: AmeriCorps*VISTA commemorates 35 years of fighting poverty in America. Since 1965, more than 130,000 VISTA members have used a hands-on, grassroots approach to empower individuals and communities throughout the country.

2001: President George W. Bush calls for a "nation of citizens, not spectators" in his inaugural address and launches faith-based and community initiative to expand support for grassroots organizations meeting local needs.

The first International Conference on Service-Learning Research is held.

The Wingspread conference on student civic engagement is held.

AmeriCorps*NCCC's San Diego campus moves to Sacramento, CA.

September 11, 2001: Terrorist attacks spark a surge of patriotism and volunteer service by Americans.

January 2002: In his state of the Union Address, President George W. Bush asks all Americans to devote two years or 4,000 hours to volunteer service during their lifetimes. As part of this call to service, he creates USA Freedom Corps, a White House office and coordinating council to encourage Americans to serve their communities and country. He also proposes to expand AmeriCorps by 50 percent.

July 2002: The Corporation awards first Homeland Security grants to engage citizens in public health, public safety, and disaster relief and preparedness.

2003: President Bush creates the President's Council on Service and Civic Participation to find ways to recognize the valuable contributions volunteers are making in our Nation. The Council creates the President's Volunteer Service Award program as a way to thank and honor Americans who, by their demonstrated commitment and example, inspire others to engage in volunteer service.

December 2003: The Bureau of Labor Statistics of the U.S. Department of Labor reports that both the number of volunteers and the volunteer rate rose over the year ended in September 2003. About 63.8 million people did volunteer work at some point from September 2002 to September 2003, up from 59.8 million for the similar period ended in September 2002.

January 2004: AmeriCorps receives record funding increase to allow programs to grow to 75,000 members.

2004: AmeriCorps*NCCC recognizes 10,000 alumni, 15.3 million service hours, 4,500 projects and 10 years of service during Legacy Weekends at all five campuses.

In recognition of its 40th anniversary, AmeriCorps*VISTA commences a study of its alumni and the impact national service had on their lives.

More than 330,000 individuals have served through AmeriCorps.

During the past decade, more than 1 billion volunteer service hours have been generated by Senior Corps volunteers.

Senior Companion Program celebrates its 30th anniversary.

More than 1.8 billion high school students participate annually in service-learning initiatives funded by Learn and Serve America.

Bibliography

Books

Banerjee, Dillon. *So, You Want to Join the Peace Corps: What to Know Before You Go*. Berkeley, Cal.: Ten Speed Press, 2000.

Boyte, Harry C., and Nancy N. Kari. *Building America: The Democratic Promise of Public Work*. Philadelphia: Temple University Press, 1996.

Buckley, William F. *Gratitude*. New York: Random House, 1990.

Clarke, Thurson. *Ask Not: The Inauguration of John F. Kennedy and the Speech That Changed America*. New York: Holt, 2004.

Cornebise, Alfred E. *The CCC Chronicles: Camp Newspapers of the Civilian Conservation Corps, 1933–1942*. Jefferson, N.C.: McFarland & Co., Inc, 2004.

Dionne, E. J., Jr., Kayla Meltzer Drogosz, and Robert E. Litan, eds. *United We Serve: National Service and the Future of Citizenship*. Washington, D.C.: Brookings Institution Press, 2003.

Eyre, Richard. *National Service: Diary of a Decade*. London: Bloomsbury, 2003.

Fiorina, Morris, and Theda Skocpol. *Civic Engagement in American Democracy*. Washington, D.C.: Brookings Institution Press, 1999.

Foley, Michael S. *Confronting the War Machine: Draft Resistance During the Vietnam War*. Chapel Hill: University of North Carolina Press, 2003.

Green, Judith. *Deep Democracy: Community, Diversity, Transformation*. Lanham, Md.: Rowman & Littlefield Publishers, 1999.

Haun, Larry. *Habitat for Humanity: How to Build a House*. Newton, Conn.: Taunton Press, 2002.

Hill, Edwin G. *In the Shadow of the Mountain: The Spirit of the CCC*. Pullman, Wash.: Washington State University Press, 1990.

Kay, Cathryn Berger. *The Complete Guide to Service Learning: Proven, Practical Ways to Engage Students in Civic Responsibility*. Minneapolis, Minn.: Free Spirit Pub., 2004.

Leonard, Paul. *Music of a Thousand Hammers: Inside Habitat for Humanity*. New York: Continuum, 2006.

Mattessich, Paul W. *Community Building: What Makes It Work*. Saint Paul, Minn.: Amherst H. Wilder Foundation, 1997.

Mattson, Kevin, and Richard C. Leone. *Engaging Youth: Combating the Apathy of Young Americans Toward Politics*. New York: Century Foundation Press, 2003.

Melzer, Richard. *Coming of Age in the Great Depression: The Civilian Conservation Corps Experience in New Mexico, 1933–1942*. Las Cruces, N.M.: Yucca Tree Press, 2000.

Pontuso, James F. *Vaclav Havel: Civic Responsibility in the Postmodern Age*. Lanham, Md.: Rowman & Littlefield, 2004.

Poplau, Ronald W. *The Doer of Good Becomes Good: A Primer on Volunteerism*. Lanham, Md: Scarecrow Education, 2004.

Putnam, Robert D. *Bowling Alone: The Collapse and Revival of American Community*. New York: Simon & Schuster, 2000.

Sachs, Jeffrey. *The End of Poverty*. New York: Penguin Press, 2005.

Sandel, Michael J. *Democracy's Discontent: America in Search of a Public Philosophy*. Cambridge, Mass.: Belknap Press of Harvard University Press, 1996.

Skocpol, Theda. *Diminished Democracy: From Membership to Management in American Civic Life*. Norman: University of Oklahoma Press, 2003.

Smith, Jason Scott. *Building New Deal Liberalism: The Political Economy of Public Works, 1933–1956*. New York: Cambridge University Press, 2006.

Sullivan, William M. *Work and Integrity: The Crisis and Promise of Professionalism in America*. New York: Harper Business, 1995.

Thomsen, Moritz. *Living Poor; a Peace Corps Chronicle*. Seattle: University of Washington Press, 1969.

Verba, Sidney. *Voice and Equality: Civic Voluntarism in American Politics*. Cambridge, Mass: Harvard University Press, 1995.

Willsea, Jennifer S., ed. *Alternatives to the Peace Corps: A Directory of Third World & U.S. Volunteer Opportunities*. 10th ed. San Francisco, Cal.: Food First Books, 2003.

Wofford, Harris. *Of Kennedys and Kings: Making Sense of the Sixties*. Pittsburgh: University of Pittsburgh Press, 1992.

Young, Richard D. *Volunteerism: Benefits, Incidence, Organizational Models, and Participation in the Public Sector*. Columbia, S.C.: University of South Carolina College of Liberal Art's Institute for Public Service and Policy Research, 2004.

Web Sites

Readers seeking additional information about national service may wish to refer to the following Web sites, all of which were operational as of this writing.

AmeriCorps

www.americorps.org

The AmeriCorps official site contains specific facts about the program and outlines its efforts in communities throughout America. The site features information on both the national and state branches of AmeriCorps, as well as its programs derived from VISTA and the Civilian Conservation Corps (see below).

Corporation for National & Community Service

www.nationalservice.org

The official Web site of the Corporation for National & Community Service offers a detailed look at the structure of community service programs in the United States today. Included are timelines of national service history, including legislative attempts to increase volunteerism, and a list of efforts undertaken to aid the victims of Hurricane Katrina.

History of the Civilian Conservation Corps

www.cccalumni.org/history1.html

A history of Franklin Delano Roosevelt's most successful and well-known national service program from its inception in 1933 to its dissolution in 1942.

Learn and Serve America

www.learnandserve.org

This site presents the efforts of Learn and Serve America, which seeks to integrate "community service projects with classroom learning."

Peace Corps

www.peacecorps.gov

The official site of the Peace Corps program includes information on the program's projects, history, and service requirements.

Peace Corps Online

peacecorpsonline.org

This unofficial Web site dedicated to providing information for returning Peace Corps volunteers features an archive of service-related information.

Senior Corps

www.seniorcorps.org

The Senior Corps engages in federal programs dedicated to organizing volunteers over the age of 55.

UN Volunteers Home Page

www.unv.org

The UN Volunteers program provides an international organization to coordinate worldwide volunteer efforts. This official Web site includes information on its programs and history.

VISTA Web

www.friendsofvista.org

Volunteers in Service to America (VISTA) seeks to alleviate the effects of poverty in both urban and rural areas. This Web site presents the history of the program and the latest news about its activities.

Additional Periodical Articles with Abstracts

More information about national service and related subjects can be found in the following articles. Readers who require a more comprehensive selection are advised to consult the *Readers' Guide Abstracts*, *Social Sciences Index*, and other H. W. Wilson publications.

Redrafting America. Terry Golway. *America*, v. 191 p7 August 2–9, 2004.

Golway writes that the division of labor has not diminished since the fall of the Roman Empire. In America, the rich, powerful, and educated are almost exempt from military service, as any look at the casualty lists from Iraq will demonstrate; the people returning home in flag-draped caskets are generally drawn from the America of diminished opportunities. The inequity of sacrifice in the war on terror has motivated some to call for a return to the draft of the World War II era, in which the rich served alongside the poor. Golway argues that the draft debate focuses on the wrong solution to America's problems abroad, however; what America needs is an army of young, idealistic people who have optimism and a sense of mission, and they are needed at home as well as abroad.

Service and the State. Tod Lindberg. *Brookings Review*, v. 20 pp38–41 Fall 2002.

Lindberg asserts that the view that national service will strengthen the ties that bind individuals into a society or create new ties is mistaken. The circumstances of different lives call for varying solutions to the problem of social connection—the impulse underlying service and charitable giving. There is no political solution to this problem, says Lindberg, only the possibility of its politicization by the state, which transforms something done to fulfill a genuine desire into something that is done to avoid sanction. If, however, people act only to avoid sanction, they will not satisfy their longing for social connection.

The Draft: An Idea Whose Time Has Come Again. Paul Magnusson. *Business Week*, p52 January 27, 2003.

Magnusson suggests that it might be a good idea to reintroduce the military draft. Democratic Representatives Charles B. Rangel (N.Y.) and John Conyers Jr. (Mich.) claim that the poor and African Americans are more likely to come home from war in body bags. According to Magnusson, Rangel and Conyers have a point when it comes to class fairness: The wealthiest 20 percent of families do not send their children to boot camp, Pentagon figures reveal. The representatives' idea is to have two years of military or public service by all men and women aged 18 to 26, with no college deferments. Among the 4 million Americans who turn 18 every year, some would enlist, while others would pick national service. The military would effectively stay a volunteer corps. Best of all, claims Magnusson, might be the effect on the nation of the shared sacrifice of its citizens.

Paved with Good Intentions. Douglas A. Hicks. *The Christian Century*, v. 119 pp10–11 July 31–August 13, 2002.

Christians should be skeptical about politicians who tout the value of voluntary service insists Hicks. In January 2001, President Bush stated that he was building on "a magnificent, courageous and compassionate response to terrorism" with the establishment of the USA Freedom Corps, an initiative that combines the AmeriCorps, Senior Corps, and Peace Corps. He then added a new group, the Citizens Corps, which will concentrate on prevention of and emergency response to terrorism. Hicks argues that Christians ought to work with Bush, other politicians, and business and civic leaders when they demonstrate a real commitment to service that is capable of improving the lives of people in need. At the same time, he says, they should also keep a critical distance from them, expect no cure-all, and be aware that an active, critical, and energetic social engagement will call for great commitment.

Draft Timeline. *Congressional Digest*, v. 83 p130 May 2004.

A guide to periods of compulsory U.S. military enrollment is presented.

National Service: Promoting a National Vision. Stephen Joel Trachtenberg. *Current*, pp32–35 December 2003.

According to Trachtenberg, the notion of national service can and will be transformational. National service, particularly military service, could address three profound issues: the need for a good counterbalance to America's healthy respect for pluralism, for a greater understanding throughout the population of what the military is and does, and to ensure that the public is protected by citizen soldiers. A national service draft, with the military as an option, says Trachtenberg, would also mean that many young people entering higher education would be better financed, motivated, and clearer about their reasons for going to college; young people would make a material contribution to society; and a renewed national cohesion could be fostered. Moreover, there may be fascinating opportunities for national service for seniors.

Public Service v. Individualism: Is There a Conflict? Alan W. Dowd. *Current*, pp13–18 February 2004.

The writer contends that Americans must find a balance between the competing forces of individualism and the greater good without expanding the size and scope of government. Today, unfettered individualism seems to have eroded the all-important connective tissue between employees and employers, shareholders and executives, neighbors and neighborhood, citizens and government, old and young. As a result, Dowd writes, the demand for rights and entitlements supersedes shared values and common responsibilities. There remains, however, an undercurrent of cooperation and community that frequently redirects the country's individualist impulse.

Global Communitarianism: An Alternative Route. Max M. Kampelman. *Current*, pp3–11 November 2005.

Kampelman explores ways in which the global development of "community" can help strengthen human development. He notes that among the original principles of the group that is now the Organization for Security and Cooperation in Europe was a series of human rights, and he argues that the United States should push for adoption of these rights by nations worldwide so as to work toward a global community of democracies. Kampelman also argues that President Bush and Russian president Putin should pledge to work toward the worldwide elimination of all nuclear weapons. He suggests that a desire for peace is now dominant among people, that the rational reasons for war are vanishing, and that globally shared human values are emerging.

The End of the Draft, and More. Stephen E. Ambrose. *National Review*, v. 51 pp35–36 August 9, 1999.

The end of conscription in 1973 may have been universally welcomed, Ambrose writes, but its absence has left a void where Americans once shared a common experience. The draft brought together Americans from all over the country, irrespective of race, class, or religion, to work toward shared goals, but now these youths discriminate among each other on the basis of their perceived entitlements. Moreover, the draft reinforced Americans' understanding of their common history and heritage. The public may be reluctant to reintroduce the draft, but the motion has been accomplished with little problem and with great success in Europe, where most youths do one year of mandatory public service upon turning 18. According to Ambrose, these teenagers, both men and women, opt for either military or community service, and a similar system could unite America as nothing else could.

Corps-Crazy. Kate O'Beirne. *National Review*, v. 54 pp24–25 February 25, 2002.

O'Beirne reports that Washington is ensuring a role for the federal government in mobilizing volunteers by launching the USA Freedom Corps. The corps, which is run out of the White House, will coordinate the activities of expanded versions of the current AmeriCorps, Senior Corps, and the Peace Corps, as well as a brand new Citizens Corps that will concentrate on domestic security. The Bush administration aims to create this new Citizen Corps, even though there is no shortage of volunteers and no apparent need for federal intervention between citizens and community groups.

Saving the Democrats. William F. Buckley. *National Review*, v. 67 p58 February 14, 2005.

Buckley suggests that Democrats should adopt the idea of columnist E. J. Dionne, a senior fellow of the Brookings Institution, that gratitude is an element of the human condition that is insufficiently acted upon. Dionne contends that the politics of gratitude is also a politics of reciprocity and generosity, because when people acknowledge the help they receive, they are more ready, individually and collectively, to help others. The idea of a national program of volunteer service could be used by the Democrats as they seek to enliven patriotism by asking that young Americans dedicate a year of their lives to demonstrating their appreciation for the obligations of mature citizenship.

Citizen Soldiers. John B. Judis. *The New Republic*, v. 220 p8 June 28, 1999.

According to Judis, the national military service program designed by Northwestern University sociologist Charles Moskos in the 1980s should be introduced. The program requires any high school graduate who seeks a federal student loan to perform either military or civilian service. In making military service an option, the program would fortify the average American family's connection to the military and forge a connection between citizenship and national obligation. It would also provide Americans of different races, nationalities, and classes with a common experience. The writer discusses the history and social and political benefits of America's now-abolished military draft system.

Slave Brigade. William A. Galston and Richard A. Posner. *The New Republic*, v. 229 July 28–August 4, 2003.

A reader responds to Judge Richard A. Posner's article "An Army of the Willing," which appeared in the May 19 issue. He takes issue with Posner's views against conscription and, in particular, his statement that "conscription could be described as a form of slavery." Posner replies.

Thinking About the Draft. William A. Galston. *The Public Interest*, pp61–73 Winter 2004.

The United States should review the decision it made 30 years ago to implement an all-volunteer armed force (AVF), contends Galston. That decision was made after the Vietnam War and has undoubtedly led to a more effective military. Unfortunately, the volunteer system has also created a belief in society that citizenship involves rights without responsibilities. There has developed what Galston calls a "spectatorial citizenship," whereby good citizens need not be active and can simply allow others to do the public's work. Finally, the AVF has helped widen the gap between the orientation and experience of military personnel and that of the citizenry as a whole. For these reasons, Galston concludes, the United States should move toward a system of universal 18-month military service for all capable high school graduates and, in the case of dropouts, all 18-year-olds.

Service Economy. Tim Cavanaugh. *Reason*, v. 33 p21 February 2002.

A recent article in the *Washington Monthly* argued for the need for a draft, but there is less to the justification than meets the eye, writes Cavanaugh. The armed forces show a distinct lack of interest in a new draft and have arguably reached a stage of professional specialization that would render conscripted troops unnecessary or problematic. In the article "Now Do You Believe We Need a Draft?," Charles Moskos and Paul Glastris suggest instead that draftees be given civilian duties as well as military ones. The writer suggests a number of humorous ways draftees could fill their time once conscripted.

Bush's Legions. Mike Lynch. *Reason*, v. 34 p17 May 2002.

Lynch interviews James Bovard, a critic of former president Clinton's AmeriCorps, a federally funded network of paid "volunteers." Bovard documented the program's follies in *Feeling Your Pain: The Explosion and Abuse of Government Power in the Clinton-Gore Years*. In this interview, he discusses such topics as the good works of the program, why Bush would want to expand it, and why it will blow up in the president's face.

American Democracy and Military Service. Morris Janowitz. *Society*, v. 35 pp39–48 January/February 1998.

In an article reprinted from 1967, Janowitz says that calls for changes in America's selective service system are based in part on the strong public presumption that the draft operates with a definite bias against the nation's lower socioeconomic groups. Although this claim contains a significant element of truth, he points out, such an image of social class bias is so oversimplified that it is an inadequate and even dangerous foundation for public discussion of the draft. The writer examines some of the social class and demographic factors involved in the impact of the selective service system and proposes an alternative, which he believes is more compatible with the requirements and aims of political democracy.

All Together Now. Margaret Carlson. *Time*, v. 159 p33 February 11, 2002.

President George W. Bush is adopting Senator John McCain's idea of expanding the national volunteer program known as AmeriCorps, reports Carlson. In his State of the Union address, Bush challenged every American to donate 4,000 hours of community service and announced a new agency called USA. Freedom Corps to organize the effort. Freedom Corps builds on existing volunteer programs and creates the Citizens Corps, a type of national Neighborhood Watch, and the Medical Reserve Corps, an army of first responders for terror attacks and other national emergencies. The new agency strikes a note that may help this indulged generation awaken to what McCain calls "a cause larger than ourselves."

Should the Draft Be Reinstated? *Time,* v. 162 pp101–102 December 29, 2003.

U.S. forces are stretched thin, says the writer, and many reservists have been called up for full-time duty, prompting some to propose a reinstatement of the draft, which opponents characterize as an unnecessary and dangerous move. Commentators on both sides of the debate present their views on the issue.

Renewing the Call to Service. David Gergen. *U.S. News & World Report,* v. 120 p76 May 10, 1996.

Gergen reports that President Clinton has asked Harris Wofford to run AmeriCorps, the umbrella organization for all federally funded volunteer and service programs. In past months, Wofford and his team set out to save AmeriCorps as well as Points of Light, former president George Bush's effort to replace the welfare state with a vibrant spirit of volunteerism, by rebuilding a base of bipartisan support for national service. Wofford asserts that the United States could make real progress if Americans could link national service to a national strategy for addressing deep-seated social needs, such as providing better schools, curbing crime and drugs, and reducing homelessness.

A Time to Heed the Call. David Gergen. *U.S. News & World Report,* v. 131 p60 December 24, 2001.

According to Gergen, the September 11 tragedy could be transformed into a mission of powerful civic engagement by the drafting of young people into national service. According to surveyors from Penn, Schoen & Berland Associates, some 81 percent of Americans would like the federal government to promote increased community and national service. They strongly support college scholarships for young people who work as police officers, firefighters, or civil-defense staff, and they want a significant enlargement of the national service program. September 11 was a defining moment for America, writes Gergen, but it will be lost if it is not grasped and given a more permanent meaning.

Society Pays Debts. Kristen Davis. *U.S. News & World Report,* v. 138 pp52–53 April 11, 2005.

Davis explains how graduate students prepared to spend a few years teaching needy children, treating patients in underserved communities, or practicing public-interest law can reduce or eliminate their graduate school debts by means of a state, federal, or private loan-repayment-assistance program. Ways in which teachers, doctors, and lawyers can have portions of their debt forgiven are discussed.

A Kinder, Gentler Draft. Craig Cox. *Utne Reader*, pp4–15 February 2002.

Cox claims that America's war on terrorism has done a great deal to rehabilitate the concept of patriotism, even among the Left. Some think it is time to set up some kind of compulsory national service as a way of institutionalizing this feeling. According to author Ann Marlowe in Salon.com, such a scheme would offer a way for young people to serve their nation while they learn the value of citizenship, discipline, and diversity. The armed forces would be merely one of a variety of options, which could incorporate everything from environmental protection and tutoring to fighting forest fires and reading to the blind. Moreover, Cox writes, unlike the Vietnam-era draft, all people of a particular age would be expected to serve, irrespective of economic or social background. The writer discusses his opposition to the plan.

A Life That Matters. Sean O'Keefe. *Vital Speeches of the Day*, v. 69 pp535–538 June 15, 2003.

At the Loyola University Commencement in New Orleans, Louisiana, on May 17, 2003, NASA administrator Sean O'Keefe, in order to make the graduates consider a future in public service, discusses the value of the commitment of two truly remarkable people: Kalpana Chawla, an immigrant to America who made the ultimate sacrifice on the space shuttle *Columbia* earlier in the year, and Admiral Stan Arthur, who retired several years ago from the navy after a 40-year career.

Keeping the Faith. Steve Waldman. *Washington Monthly*, v. 33 pp18–19 October 2001.

On May 21, President George W. Bush unveiled his faith-based initiative to give federal support to religious organizations that give services to the needy. When he announced his plans, he mentioned three initiatives. The first was a change in the tax code to give charitable deductions to those who do not itemize their tax returns, an idea that was quickly shelved to ensure that enough money would be available for the rest of his tax cut. The second was a proposal to give grants to religious groups to help them do good works, which may become law in a much more modest form. The third idea was that national service should be some part of the mix. The writer discusses the part AmeriCorps could play in realizing this final idea.

First Draft. Paul Glastris. *Washington Monthly,* v. 35 pp11–13 March 2003.

The draft may not be the type of political loser that it is believed to be by the majority of Beltway observers, asserts Glastris. Virtually every argument against the draft boils down to the belief that it is not truly needed for the defense of the United States, but history belies the notion that a draft can only be passed in the case of an overwhelmingly obvious need. There are fundamental flaws in the all-volunteer force, he says, as evidenced by the fact that the military is experiencing serious difficulties in meeting recruitment targets without reducing standards. Although defenders of the all-volunteer force believe that the military can solve these problems by recruiting more troops with increased pay and improved benefits, this is becoming more and more difficult to achieve. A 21st-century draft should be devised, insists Glastris, in a way that would help resolve the current weaknesses without undermining its strengths. Although many young people would be opposed to such a draft, none would have reason to feel that their peers were receiving an unequitable head start in their careers.

Index

Abrams, Creighton, 74
Ackerman, Bruce, 152
ACTION agency, 24, 171
Adams, Henry, 93–94
Afghanistan, 75
Alstott, Anne, 152
America's Promise Alliance, 18
AmeriCorps
    about, 108, 111
    expansion, 37–38, 124, 124–125, 151
    funding/costs, 120, 121–122, 124–125, 138, 142–143, 158
    history, 17, 36, 173–175
    hurricane relief, 110–112
    impact, 138
    long-term civic effects, 107–108
    participation levels, 19, 140
    presidential calls to service and, 24–25
    service delivery model, 33, 143
    volunteer recruitment, 28, 32
Annan, Kofi, 117
antipoverty programs, 10–12, 14
armies of compassion, 30, 32
ASC (American Association of State Service Commissions), 174
Asch, Beth, 38

Bailey, Bruce, 111
Bayh, Evan, 159
    See also McCain-Bayh bill
Bellak, Sarah, 109
Bellamy, Carol, 118
Bennett, Drake, 151–154
Berger, Peter, 30
Bosnia, 71, 73, 75
Boys and Girls Clubs, 18
Bridgeland, John, 29–34
Briery, David, 113–115
British Columbia, 135
Brooks, David, 36–38, 154
Brown University, 15

Brown, Jerry, 172
Brown, Marian Gail, 99–100
Brown, Mark Malloch, 118
Brown, Michael, 137–138
Brundtland, Gro Harlem, 118
Buckley, William, 159
Bullard, Don, 120
Burke, Tracy, 131–132
Bush administration
    civic agenda, 29–34, 119–120, 124–125, 151
    on conscription, 65–66
    war against Iraq and, 69–70
Bush, George H. W., 7, 16, 24, 138, 157–158, 172–173
Bush, George W.
    call for civic engagement, 25, 115, 155
    civic engagement effects, 139
    federal service programs, 20, 124–125, 138, 174
    on military readiness, 75
Bush, Laura, 20

Cal State Monterey Bay, 131–134
California, 14
California Conservation Corps, 172
California Performance Review, 131–132
Campus Compact, 15, 19, 172
Campus Outreach Opportunity League, 172
capacity building, 32
Capeling-Alakija, Sharon, 118
Carlson, Danielle, 97
Carter, Jimmy, 14, 24
Carter, Phillip, 69–81
Cato Institute, 35
CCC (Civilian Conservation Corps), 10, 14, 157, 170
Chapman, Bruce, 142, 145–150
charitable organizations, 48
Chase, Eric, 114–115
Chase, Gail, 114–115
Chicago, 7

CIRCLE study, 153
Citizen Corps, 29
Citizen Service Act of 2002, 33
City Year, 16, 124
civil rights movement, 13
Clinton administration, 75, 154
Clinton, Bill
    call for civic engagement, 155
    civic agenda, 16, 18, 24, 138
    federal service programs, 36, 157, 173
    student aid, 15
Cole, Steven, 113–114
colleges, 5–21, 25–26, 80–81, 131–134
communitarianism, 82–86
community service programs
    history, 15, 18–20, 170–175
    long-term civic effects, 107–108
    participation levels, 34
    recruitment, 26–28
    See also specific programs
compulsory national service. *See* universal national service
Conconi, Bill, 135–136
conscription
    alternatives, 75–79
    arguments against, 79, 93–94, 145–146, 148
    arguments for, 67–68, 70, 79–80
    as commodification, 84–86
    Bush administration on, 65–66
    college/university admission and, 80–81
    in Germany, 87–88
    motives examined, 160–162
    political divide, 102
    Vietnam war impact, 74
    youth and, 95–98, 99–100, 101–102
    See also universal national service
contractors, military, 76, 164–165
Cook, John, 95–98
Cornuelle, Richard, 30, 163
corporate sector, 45–46, 164
Corporation for National and Community Service, 16–17, 19, 24, 28, 173

Daily Points of Light Award, 174
Dang, Jacob, 114
Daniels, Sarah, 113
Davis, Clara, 99–100
Davis, Gray, 132
Davis, Victor Hanson, 85
Delli Carpini, Michael, 154
development cooperation programs, 116–118
Dewey, John, 170
DLC (Democratic Leadership Council), 35
Donahue, Kate, 107
Dowd, Alan, 155–166

Eckhardt, Season, 133
educational institutions
    history of civic engagements, 5–21
    service-learning courses, 25–26, 131–132
    universal national service and, 80–81, 131–134, 135–136, 147, 150, 153
Eggers, Dave, 121, 123–125, 152
Ehrlich, Thomas, 153
826 Valencia program, 123
Eisner, David, 19, 107–108

Faherty, John, 113–115
federal service programs
    history, 7–21, 170–175
    long-term civic effects, 107–108
    participation levels, 34
    public service definition and, 158–159
    voluntary sector and, 30–34
    See also specific programs
Fong, Cheryl, 133
Ford Foundation, 12, 14
Foster Grandparent Program, 170–174
France, 87
Freedom Corps. *See* USA Freedom Corps
Friedman, Max, 93–94
Fuller, Millard, 32

Garb, Sarah, 123
Germany, 87–88
GI Bill, 137–138, 144, 170
Glastris, Paul, 35, 38, 69–81
Global Youth Service Day, 19
Gold, Philip, 146
Goldsmith, Stephen, 29–34
Goodwin, Robert, 17
Grant, Christiane, 97

Gregory, Alicia, 131, 134
Gulf War, 73, 75, 140
Gulli, Cathy, 135–136
Gutierrez, Jose Antonio, 156

Habansky, Jesse, 100
Habitat for Humanity, 19, 24, 32–33, 107
Hagel, Chuck, 101
Hammack, David, 38
"Hands Across America", 24
Head Start program, 13
Hemly, James, 72
Hesburgh, Father, 14
Hollander, Liz, 19
homeland security, 140–141, 145
Hurricane Katrina, 137
hurricane relief efforts, 110–112
Hutchins, Robert, 7

individualism, 155–156, 162
international cooperation programs, 8–10, 43–44, 47–48, 116–118
International Year of Volunteers (IYV), 39–41, 117
Israel, 146, 147

James, William, 6–7, 151, 157, 170
Jehn, Christopher, 93–94
Job Corps, 10, 170–171
Johnson, Lyndon, 10–11, 23, 157, 170
Jones, Malcolm, 110–112
Just, Richard, 35–38

Karabell, Zachary, 86
Kelly, Marsha, 111
Kennedy, Edward, 16
Kennedy, John
    call for civic engagement, 23, 155
    federal service programs, 7–10, 138, 157, 169, 170
    on liberty, 73
Kennedy, Robert, 13
Kenya, 116–117
Kerry, John, 77, 102
Khazei, Alan, 137–138
King, David, 86
King, Martin Luther, 13
Korea, 73
Kosovo, 71, 73, 75
Kristol, William, 154

Lang, Eugene, 19

Lawson, Jerry, 112
Learn and Serve America, 24, 27, 173
Leebaert, Derek, 160, 162
legislation
    framework laws, 49–50
    government role, 54–55
    history, 173
    impact on volunteerism, 43–49
    overview, 39, 41–43
    recommendations, 55–56
Leiser, Ken, 110–112
Lenkowsky, Leslie, 28, 29–34
Lewis, Josh, 110
liability issues, 45, 136
liberalism, 82, 132
Light, Paul, 23–28
Lind, Michael, 84
Lindsay, John, 12
Litan, Robert, 139–144, 145, 146, 147, 148
Litow, Stanley, 12

Make a Difference Day, 19
mandatory national service. *See* universal national service
Marotti, Giancarlo, 99
Marshall, George C., 10
Marshall, Will, 35–38
Martin Luther King Day, 19, 173
Mason, Ashley, 97
McCain, John, 36, 119–120, 121–122, 159
McCain-Bayh bill, 35, 37–38, 120, 158–159
McCurdy, David, 16
mediating structures, 30
military contractors, 76, 164–165
military forces
    active vs. reserve units, 66, 71, 74, 78–79
    demographics, 67, 74, 79, 85, 97, 160, 161
    enlistment levels, 65–66, 72
    GI Bill, 137–138, 144, 170
    manpower solutions, 75–79
    public image of, 84–85, 86
    size requirements, 70–73, 77
    universal national service, 38
    war on Iraq impact, 67–68, 69–75, 81, 140
    See also conscription

military reform, 76
Mill, John Stuart, 82
Mondale, Walter, 14
Moskos, Charles, 35–38, 95–98

Nachtwei, Winfried, 87
National and Community Service Trust Act of 1993, 173
National Association of Service and Conservation Corps (NASCC), 15, 172
National Center for Voluntary Action, 24
National Civilian Community Corps, 173–174
National Service Act of 1990, 16
national service timeline, 170–175
National Service-Learning Conference, 19
National Student Association (NSA), 8
National Teacher Corps, 170
National Youth Service Day, 19
Naumann, Klaus, 88
Naval forces, 76
Neuhaus, Richard John, 30
New York City, 12, 13
New York University (NYU), 11
Newfoundland, 135
Nisbet, Robert, 30
Niskanen, William, 149
Nixon, Richard, 23–24, 160
Noah, Timothy, 36
nonprofit sector
    careers in, 27, 109
    civic agenda, 30
    federal service programs and, 33
    legal frameworks for, 48
    participation levels, 34
Northwest Territories, 135
Nunavut, 135
Nunn, Sam, 16

Ontario, 135
overseas programs. *See* international cooperation programs
Owens, Mackubin, 161

parental socialization, 26
Paterson, Tony, 87–88
Paul, Ron, 93
Peace Corps
    about, 114–115
    history, 8–10, 13, 23, 170–171

JFK Executive Order, 169
    participation levels, 19, 108, 113–115, 138, 140
Peck, Fred, 160
Peterson, Megan, 123
Pew Foundation, 14
Points of Light Foundation, 16–18, 19, 24, 172
Pollack, Seth, 131, 133
Posner, Richard, 82–86
Powell, Colin, 17, 70, 74, 174
President's Council on Service and Civic Participation, 175
President's Volunteer Service Award, 175
presidential calls to service, 23–28, 115, 138
    See also specific presidents
Presidents' Summit for America's Future (1997), 17 19, 24, 174
private sector. *See* corporate sector
Project Pericles, 19
public service, 155–166
Putnam, Robert, 30, 83, 141

Raham, Helen, 136
Rajendran, Dushyandi, 135–136
Ramm, Colette, 117
RAND Corporation analysis, 70–71
Rangel, Charles, 67–68, 85, 161
Reagan, Ronald, 15, 24
Reed, Stephen, 131
Rizzitelli, J. P., 100
role models, 98
Romney, George, 15, 17–18, 21
Roosevelt, Franklin D., 10, 157, 170
Rose, Adam, 110
RSVP (Retired Senior Volunteer Program), 15, 170–174
Rumsfeld, Donald, 65–66, 70
Rwanda, 73

Sallee, Marguerite, 18
Sanchez, Julian, 121–122
Sandel, Michael, 84–85
Schinder, Dannah, 97
schools. *See* educational institutions
Schroder, Gerhard, 87
Schwarzenegger, Arnold, 131, 133
Scott, Sandy, 108
Senior Companion Program, 170–175
Senior Corps, 24, 170, 173, 175
Sept. 11 attacks

civic engagement effects, 31, 95–96, 119, 137, 139–140, 151, 175
universal national service and, 37
Serma, Marissa, 134
Shaw, George Bernard, 164
Sheriff, Leslie, 136
Shinseki, Eric, 70, 71
Shriver, Sargent, 8–12
Slater, Eric, 131–134
social welfare laws, 46–47, 54
socioeconomic status, 67, 74, 79, 85, 97, 160
Sowell, Thomas, 132
Spiller, Candace, 120
Stoneman, Dorothy, 15
Student Nonviolent Coordinating Committee (SNCC), 13
subsistence benefits, 46–47, 51–53, 54
Summers, Lawrence, 152

Talbert, Abraham, 120
Tarrant, David, 107–109
tax laws, 46
Teach for America, 123–124
Tocqueville, Alexis de, 30, 154, 155, 163
Trutna, Tiana, 131
tutoring programs, 123

unilateral action, 76
UNISTAR volunteers, 116
United Nations Volunteer Program (UNV), 116–118
universal national service
    arguments against, 143, 145–150, 151–154
    arguments for, 137–138, 139–144
    educational institutions and, 80–81, 131–134, 135–136, 147, 150, 153
    overview, 35–38
    public service definition and, 155–166
    See also conscription
Universal National Service Act of 2003, 93, 99, 101
universities, 5–21, 25–26, 80–81, 131–134
University of California, 132–133
University of Chicago, 6–7
University of Michigan, 8
University of Notre Dame, 9
University Year of Action, 170
Urban Corps, 12, 171

USA Freedom Corps, 20, 29, 33, 175

Van Til, Jon, 37
Vietnam War
    demographics, 160, 161
    history of civic engagement and, 12–13, 23
    military force deployment, 73
    military image and, 86
    military/civilian culture gap, 138
    motivation of soldiers in, 94
    "total force" concept and, 74
VISTA (Volunteers in Service to America), 10–12, 17, 23, 32–33, 170–174
volunteer organizations
    federal service programs and, 32–34
    framework laws, 52–54
    politics and, 152
    recruitment, 27–28
volunteer service
    expense reimbursement, 51–53
    federal service programs and, 30–34
    forms of, 40–42
    framework laws, 49–56
    history, 15, 170–175
    legislation impact, 43–49
    liability issues, 45, 136
    participation levels, 34, 164
    presidential endorsements, 23–28
    recognition of, 53–54
    recruitment, 26–28

Wagner, Josh, 97
war against Iraq
    international rift, 87
    military resources impact, 67–68, 69–75, 81, 140
    public response, 84–85, 99–100
war on poverty, 10–12, 170
war on terrorism, 140, 152, 162
Weddington, Susan, 108–109
Weinberger, Caspar, 74
Welch, Dennis, 101–102
welfare benefits, 46–47, 54
White, Thomas, 70, 71
Williams, Elzela, 110, 112
Wittman, Marshall, 36–38
Wofford, Harris, 5–22

Work Projects Administration, 170
World War I, 73
World War II, 73, 162

Young Adult Conservation Corps, 172
Youniss, James, 135
youth
    as apolitical, 153
    conscription and, 95–98, 99–100, 101–102
    history of civic engagement, 5–21
    service-learning courses, 25–26, 131–132
    universal national service and, 80–81
Youth Conservation Corps, 171
Youth Engaged in Service (YES), 16
Youth Service America, 172
Youth-Build, 15
Yukon, 135